Do It Right! 101 Solutions for Discipline Dilemmas

Maryln Appelbaum

ISBN# 978-0-9819625-3-5

Printed in the United States of America by
Appelbaum Publishing Company 800-23-CHILD

Do It Right!
101 Solutions for Discipline Dilemmas

by Maryln Appelbaum

TABLE OF CONTENTS

Preface

Knowing the best discipline strategies has always been tough. But now, the world is a different place than ever before. There are more children who are strong-willed. Bullying is reaching an all-time high with the advent of the internet and cell phones. The internet, cell phones, and social media have introduced a whole new generation of tech-savvy kids who sometimes text their parents rather than speaking to them even if they are in the same room.

Teen pregnancies have escalated. School drop-outs are increasing. Violence and mean kids in schools are on the rise. Never before did students have to go through a security screening just to enter their schools to be sure they don't carry weapons.

The 2 R's, respect and responsibility, seem to belong to a different age. This book is designed to help restore those 2 R's back into homes and schools. It is packed with strategies that are effective. You will receive strategies for all children, all ages. There are multiple strategies throughout the book rather than just one or two for a particular misbehavior. The reason for that is because all children are different. What works for one child, may not work for another child. Not only are children different, but so too are adults. What comes easily for you may not come as easily to another adult. You will read this book and when you get to some strategies, you will nod your head, and say, "I want to try this one right away."

This book is designed to give you skills you need to restore the 2 R's, respect and responsibility, to take charge in your home or classroom, and to have improved relationships with children.

I dedicate this book to my son and business partner, Marty Appelbaum. Together, we strive daily to make a difference in the lives of children.

Introduction

Each child is like a tiny seedling planted deeply within the ground of life. The little seedling needs to be watered, to be fed, and to receive sunlight in order to blossom and grow. It needs a healthy environment, one in which the soil is rich and fertile. It needs just the right amount of caring and nurturing of light and rain. Too much or too little sunlight and water will cause it to wilt. Children are like seedlings planted deeply within the soil. How they are watered, fed, and cared for determines how they grow.

Taking care of children is a sacred task, one that is more important than any other in society. There is no job that can compare with the importance of preparing children for the world. Children are the future. How they are nurtured and guided determines the adults that they become. The adults that they become will determine the world that will be. Will children be self-disciplined? Will they be kind? Will they be leaders? Will they have strength and endurance? Will they have courage? These are all traits that you can help them to have — with your caring and your love.

Today, there are more "strong-willed" children more challenging children, more disrespectful children and more children with special needs than ever before. This book is designed to help you with all children.

Do you remember when you first learned to drive a car? There was so much to learn. You had to learn the parts of the car that were relevant to driving--the steering wheel, brakes, turn signals, gas tank, and so much more. Then, you had to practice and practice until you could naturally get into a car, start to drive, and not have to think about it. That is how raising children must work, too. First, you have to have basic knowledge and skills, and then lots of practice.

Sure, you can get into a car without knowledge and practice and drive it away. It will be rocky, but you will be able to drive. You may get into some accidents. You may cause yourself to get hurt. Worse, you may cause others to be hurt. So too, can you raise children. You can give birth and just "drive." But without proper knowledge and practice, it will be rocky. You may accidentally go into reverse, brake too soon, and put the wrong ingredients into the gas tank. The vehicle that will rock will be more than a machine. It will be your child.

Children deserve more. They deserve for you to know what you are doing. They deserve a steady ride. They deserve to have a developmentally appropriate environment. That is the intent of this book. It is designed to give you the knowledge and skills that you need to do the best you possibly can. It is written to help you to drive with a steady foot. It is the guide for you to have the discipline techniques you need so you can have more confidence and know that you are doing it right.

You deserve to feel successful, to experience the thrill of seeing children step out into the world fully nurtured and fully successful, and to know that you have played your part well.

This book can totally change your life. Moreover, it can transform your children's lives, too. It will be up to you how much of a change this will be. The more often you read the book, and the more often you do the exercises, the more effective your learning will be.

Take lots of time to read it thoroughly. Give yourself a chance to thoroughly absorb what you read. Do each quiz and re-check your answers until you always receive 100% every time. Don't "short change" yourself or your children.

If you are reading this book and are a child care professional working daily with children, watch the difference as you begin to implement the techniques taught in this book. Tell your parents about the techniques that you will be learning. Invite them to support you by using the same techniques at home. Share this book with them. This book benefits everyone who has children in their care.

Thank you for wanting to learn and grow. Thank you for using this book as the instrument for your growth in child caring skills. You are on your way to learning how to do it right with positive discipline and guidance.

About the Author

Maryln Appelbaum is well known internationally as an outstanding authority on children, education, and families. She has Master's degrees in both psychology and education and completed her doctoral studies in both education and psychology. She has worked as a teacher, an administrator, and a therapist, and has been a consultant throughout the United States. She has written more than thirty "how to" books geared exclusively for educators and parents. She is frequently interviewed as an expert on television and radio talk shows.

She owns the seminar training company, Appelbaum Training Institute, with her son, Marty Appelbaum. They and their speakers train educators and parents all over the world. Maryln's influence impacts the entire globe with her thoughts for the day, which go out daily to thousands of educators via e-mail. Her strategies have been successfully implemented in homes and schools across the world. There is not a day that goes by that someone does not contact her at Appelbaum Training Institute to tell her thank you. Those thank-you's come from people all over the globe whose lives have been impacted by Maryln. Maryln's books and talks are always packed with strategies for success. She is a positive, motivational, dynamic, caring, one-of-a-kind difference maker for the world.

A DISCIPLINE CHECKLIST

Here is a fun exercise for you to check what you know. Quickly go through the statements and mark each one with a "T" for True or an "F" for False. These are topics in which you will become an "EXPERT" by the time you have completed this training book.

_____ 1. Discipline teaches correct behaviors.

_____ 2. Discipline punishes the child.

_____ 3. It is important to think positively about children even when they are exhibiting extremely negative behaviors.

_____ 4. When administering discipline, the adult is frustrated and angry.

_____ 5. After punishment, children feel secure and have a better understanding of themselves.

_____ 6. Punishment teaches the child how to deal with feelings.

_____ 7. It is important to always use the same discipline technique for all situations so you are consistent.

_____ 8. It is not important to be consistent.

_____ 9. The child's greatest need is to make his or her own decisions.

_____ 10. There are never too many hugs, too much love, or too much praise that can be given to a child.

_____ 11. When the adult yells, children know they better listen.

_____ 12. The child will understand discipline better if the adult is angry when administering the discipline.

_____ 13. It is important that the bedtime of children varies according to the needs of the parent.

_____ 14. It is important to praise children even when the praise isn't sincere.

_____ 15. Using the word "bad" when talking to a child, can cause a child's self-esteem to suffer.

Chapter **1**

The Needs of Children

In addition to physical and safety needs, children have very important emotional needs that must be met in order for them to feel secure. When these needs are appropriately met, children behave better and there are less discipline problems. Pay special attention to these needs if you have a child that appears to need lots of attention. That child most probably has at least one of these needs not being fulfilled. Fill the need and watch the problem disappear.

Love

Love is a vital force for living. It can give you the strength to go on no matter what the circumstances are around you. There are songs, books, movies, and plays written about love. When you feel loved, you feel good all over. You feel like you are important. You feel cared about. You feel worthwhile. When you don't feel loved, you feel lonely, isolated, and insecure. Worse, you may feel like there is something wrong with you because no one loves you. It is the same with children. They must feel loved to thrive and flourish. They must feel loved to feel worthwhile and capable. I cannot think of a time that love is not important for children. I have seen children who have been badly abused by their parents, and they still crave love from their parents.

Children need love starting in infancy. They need to feel that there is someone there, someone who loves them, someone they can always count on. This continues through not only their elementary years, but their adolescent years and also as adults.

There are many ways to show love to children. One way is through appropriate physical touch. It's great to get a pat on the back, a hug, or a gentle squeeze on the arm. This is the kind of touch that shows clearly to children that they are cared about.

Another great way to show children that they are loved is through eye contact. It has been said that, "the eyes are the windows to the soul," and it appears to be true. You can say so very much to children by looking at them lovingly. You can feel so much back by the way that they look at you. Start now to use your eyes to show your children that you believe in them, that you truly care.

I am a people watcher, and for me it is a delight to watch parents look at their children lovingly. I love the way parents look at their newborns with awe and wonder and love. I love to see the pride in their eyes when they see their teens graduate. It's that shining pride that children also see in their parents' eyes that tells them they are loved.

An easy wonderful way to show love is to smile when you look at children. Let them see you grinning from ear to ear with delight as you listen to them talk or watch them engage in something new. Let them know that you are happy to have them. This is a great gift of love to give to your children.

Acceptance is a great way to show children that they are loved. Acceptance means accepting all parts of the child, not just the parts that you like. The child is a whole package, just as you are a whole package. He or she will have good days and poor days. You have that, too! Don't you want to be loved on the "poor days?" Those are the days that you need the love even more. So too, do children. Those are the days that you have to make even more of an effort to show children you care.

Acceptance means never saying that the child is "bad." That word needs to be erased from your vocabulary. If you tell a child that he or she is BAD, the child will begin to believe it. The child who believes that he or she is bad, will act the part, will become that way. The only way to switch it off is to believe in the child always, no matter what is going on.

It is not always easy to accept some children. There are times when you may feel frustrated, angry, and even hurt. You can still accept and love the child. You may not be pleased with the child's behaviors, but it is not the child's behaviors that you love. It is the child's essence--the child's individual spirit that is so very individual and unique. This is what you need to nurture and develop. When you accept children, you help them feel important and loved.

Sincere compliments are another way to show children they are loved. It is important that children hear when they do things that are appropriate. I had one child say to me, "My teacher tells me everything I do wrong, but never anything I do right." That teacher probably thought that criticism would help the child, but instead it made the child give up.

> *"Thank you so much."*
> *"Thanks for remembering to do that."*
> *"I'm so glad to see you today."*
> *"What a joy it is to have you here with me."*

Those are statements that can inspire and uplift children to be all they can be. These are so much better than negative statements that deplete the child's self-worth.

The best compliments are spontaneous. It just pours forth from you like a river flooding both you and the child with good feelings. Say things sincerely. Point out positive characteristics and actions.

Compliment specific appropriate behaviors that children do. "I like the way you put your toys away." "I loved the way you were so kind to Jamie." "Thank you for sharing your lunch with Tommy."

Try to remember to not let any day go by without saying something loving to each child at least once. I know parents who have a bedtime ritual each night telling their children all the things they love about them. This is a great way to go to sleep. This is a great esteem booster for children. Children who have good self-esteem feel worthwhile. They don't need to act out to get attention. They are getting all the attention they need in appropriate ways.

A benefit is that the more positive you are and the more you encourage and compliment children, the more you will see them doing the same thing to their peers and others in the family. What a great day you will have when one of your children spontaneously compliments you.

A very important way to show children that you love them is to listen to them. Listen to them when they are feeling good, and also listen to them when they don't feel good. Listen without judgment to what they have to say. The best way to listen is to simply nod your head and say words like "Really," "Aha," "Would you like to tell me more?"

Acknowledge how the child is feeling with words like, "Sounds like that made you sad."   Another way to show children that you love them is to give them the gift of "time." Take time to really enjoy children. Take time to listen, to love, to laugh, and to cry with your children. This is a world in which people are rushing about trying to achieve dreams, trying to make ends meet, trying to "get it all done." What sometimes is left out, is spending time with children, the hope for the future. Children feel this lack. They need you. They need you to spend time with them and help them feel loved and important.

Kimi's parents were both busy all the time. Kimi's mom had an important high-tech job and had to work late sometimes. Her dad was in sales and traveled a lot. They both loved Kimi, but were often exhausted by the end of the day. All they could think about was eating something, watching a little TV, and going to bed. Kimi wanted her time, too. She started having bedtime issues. She would cry every night when they put her to sleep. She would cry so long, that eventually, they would give up, and just bring her in their bed. She cried at dinner time, so they let her eat whatever she wanted. Nothing they seemed to do was enough, and the truth was that it really wasn't.

What Kimi really wanted was quality time with her parents. They came to one of my workshops, and learned about the importance of spending time with Kimi. They each started scheduling weekly dates with her. She had her Daddy Date one night a week. They went somewhere special to eat. She got to choose the restaurant. They spent about an hour there, and Kimi would talk while her dad listened. She also had a Mommy Date once a week. During that time, it was just the two of them. They played games, did cooking projects, or made gifts for holidays. It was their special time to have fun. Every night at bedtime, they each spent alone time with Kimi for a few minutes while she talked about the highlights of her day. It was their special time. Soon, Kimi started behaving better. She didn't need to misbehave for attention. She was getting lots of loving time, and that was what she really wanted.

You have probably heard people say that it's the quality of time that you spend with loved ones this important. It takes lots of quantity time before you can have quality time. It takes time for children to feel safe, and for them to feel that their time with you is really sacred. That is when they open up and share with you. That quantity of time sets the tone for quality time that sets the tone for a long-lasting relationship with your children.

> ## *It takes lots of quantity time before you can have quality time.*

Order

Children have a need for order in their lives that is as strong as their need for love. They need to have structure so that they feel secure. When their lives are disorderly, they behave the same way. Children are not going to tell you, "I need order." Their behaviors will probably reflect the opposite. Yet they scream out for it. Change the meal time or bedtime, take a child on an unfamiliar outing, bring a new child into the child's environment, or be gone for a day and chaos will erupt. They need sameness, consistency, and routine.

Their minds are constantly absorbing everything that is happening in their environment. They want to learn everything at once. In the midst of all this natural tumult of growing, they must have a sense of what is going to happen in their lives. This is where you step in with order.

There are many ways that you can give children order. First and foremost, have a schedule. Things need to happen at the same time each day. Children need to know that they will be eating at the same time, playing at the same time, sleeping at the same time, even brushing their teeth at the same time.

Children can't tell time by looking at a clock. They have their own internal clocks. The best way that you can help set that clock is by the "routine" that you make part of the schedule. For example, young children have lunch, clean up, go to the bathroom, have a quiet story, and then quietly lay down for a nap. That is the routine, the schedule. This can't vary. The story can vary, what the children eat for lunch can vary, but the basic schedule needs to stay the same.

Older children need that same sense of structure. Teens especially need this. Their hormones may be raging, and they may feel like they are unpredictable. They need you to be predictable. This is a time when they are pondering their identities. They may even go through a phase where they think their parents are old-fashioned, and that they have the right answers. In their hearts, they still need structure. They need a set time to do their homework. They need curfews when they go out in the evening. If they have an allowance, it is best if it is earned through responsibilities they have in the home.

You can best fulfill the need for order by the way that you act. You are a role model for your children at all times. You are teaching, even when you wish you were not. They are watching you and copying you. You are a role model. This learning will stick with them longer than the learning they get through computers and books.

Be consistent. When you say something and don't follow through, that creates disorder for children. They need to know that you mean what you say. They need to feel your strength and your power so that they will learn to have that same strength and power.

When you say to a child, "No dessert unless you eat your vegetables," follow through. If you follow through one day, and the next day you waiver, they don't learn about order. Instead, they are learning another concept, and that is how to get what they want through manipulation. It's important that you do not teach this to your children. If you don't follow through, children never know what to expect, so they will try and try and try to get something else. The more that you waiver and are inconsistent, the more they will manipulate. The more that they manipulate and get what they want, the more they will think that they can always get what they want from others. This is not preparing them for the real world. They can get what they want in life, but it is from setting goals and learning how to work toward those goals. Teach them to respect you and what you say. Teach them that you do not waiver. Teach them that you do know what you want and that you follow through to get it. Let them learn to respect you. Let them see you as a strong and powerful role model for them.

It takes courage and strength to be consistent. Most adults worry that their children won't love them or like them if they are consistent. Being consistent isn't the same as being mean. It is instead, an important manner to meet your children's need for order. They will love and respect you even more, even though they seem to rebel. That's because it is a change for them. It's being inconsistent from the way you have been behaving. It will take a little time for them to adjust to your new behavior. They will adjust. They will soon learn that when you say something, you mean it. Their lives will have order, and you will have provided it.

What about you? How do you look? How do you act? Is your life with your children orderly? Do you take time to comb your hair neatly? Are your clothes neat and clean? What about your hands and nails? You are teaching children at all times. For your own sake, it is important to look orderly, to take time for yourself each day in grooming yourself. If you like the way you look, you will feel better. You will feel more important. You will demonstrate that you care about you. The children will sense this and have more respect for you.

The physical environment of children needs to be orderly, too. Everything needs to have its own special place. When there is a place for everything, children learn exactly where to go to find what they want.

Everything needs to be orderly.

Storage areas for children in their rooms and throughout the house need to be orderly. Shelves for toys and learning materials are great for young children. Items that are kept on the shelves can each be kept in a certain place. Does the child want to play with the "train puzzle?" The child knows that it is on the third shelf all the way over on the right. That is where the child will return the puzzle when he or she has completed it. The puzzle is always in the same place. There is a sense of security for children to know that if they want it, they know exactly where to find it.

The same holds true with older children. Their rooms are often messy, and they can't find anything, but they sure always know where their cell phones are. Help them to have their rooms organized so that they can easily find things.

Storage places also need to be neat. Children learn more from what they see *YOU DO,* then from what you tell them. Therefore, keep everything neat and tidy and your children will keep everything neat and tidy.

Wisdom

Children love to have heroes. They want someone to look up to, to respect, who has answers when they need it. When they don't have those heroes in real life, they look to sport figures, television, and movie stars to be their heroes. It's important that they have real life heroes, people they esteem and respect. Your goal is to be that person for the children in your life. Have you ever noticed that YOU are that someone. You may feel at times that you don't have the answers. However, you do have more answers and more wisdom than the child does by the sheer fact that you are an adult. You are also an intelligent adult, or you wouldn't be able to read this and do the exercises.

Children's need for heroes and role models is evidenced by their love of super heroes on television. They copy these "heroes." It's important that you are the role model for your children, the person that they will like so much that they will want to copy.

Use your wisdom. Teach your children by having answers for them. If you don't know the answers, search them out, find them, or better yet, teach your children how to find the answers. That's a greater wisdom. That's the wisdom of teaching your children to do things for themselves so that they can become independent fully-functioning adults.

Demonstrate your wisdom by not being afraid to be in charge. Your children need you to be in charge. They aren't ready for that responsibility, yet. They will learn about being in charge by watching you. When you are in charge, you give them comfort. There is someone that they trust who has answers.

Have you ever been to an outstanding workshop with an outstanding teacher, a teacher who took charge? What a great feeling it is to have a teacher, a leader, whom you can respect. A teacher who tells you exactly what to expect, and then it happens! The teacher is in charge, yet includes you. You feel important. It makes you more eager to learn. So too, must you be with your children, whatever environment you are in, you must be a leader and in charge.

Being wise means BELIEVING IN YOURSELF. How can your children believe in you and what you say if you don't believe in yourself? If you don't believe in yourself your children will intuitively know it, and they will "play you like a bouncing ball." They will be "bouncing you!" Someone has to be in charge in every situation, and if you don't take charge, then your children will. They are not ready for that power, for that authority; someday they will be, and it will come from watching and learning from you.

Believe in yourself. Believe that you are worthwhile. Believe that you have the strength to be with children, to love children, to want to teach children. Believe in your importance. You are important. You have one of the most important jobs in the world. Think about it! Your job involves all of the most essential professional skills. There are times that you have to have the diplomacy of a lawyer, the counseling skills of a psychologist, the healing skills of a nurse, and the teaching skills of a college professor.

You are important. You are needed. You are paving the way for a new generation with your children. You are on the foreground of a whole new society by the way that you teach.

Boundaries

Boundaries are rules and limitations. They teach children specifically what it is that you expect. They also fulfill your children's need for order in a loving way. Children need to know the rules. Within those rules, they need to have freedom to "be" and to explore, but the basic structure of rules lays the framework for your children.

They need to know the areas of the environment that are taboo. For example, young children may not be allowed into the kitchen without an adult. Once in the kitchen, they cannot open the refrigerator or the stove or cabinets. Those belong to you. They have their own areas that belong to them. This is a rule, a limit, a boundary for your children. As they grow older, this area is now "on-limits." They are old enough to go into the kitchen, cook, make snacks, and help themselves to treats. Another area that may be taboo may be your office. That may stay taboo regardless of the age of children. You set your own areas that are taboo.

There are some things that are sometimes taboo and other times; they are open to the children. This is confusing for children. A fun way to handle this is to use the traffic signal approach. To use this traffic signal approach, you have colored signs that look like traffic signals. Use a red crayon to outline the red light, a yellow crayon to outline the yellow light,

and a green crayon to outline the green light. Teach the children that red means stop. It means do not touch. Show them a traffic signal with the red light completely filled in with red crayon. Explain how cars have to stop when the light is red, and they do too.

Show them a traffic signal with the green light completely filled in with a green crayon. Explain that cars can go when they have a traffic light that is green. Tell them that a green light means that they have permission to go, also. They can touch the item or go into the room. The signal will be hanging where they can see it.

Show them a traffic light with the yellow circle filled in. Explain that when they see the yellow light that it means to ask your permission.

The traffic lights are good for younger children. For older children and teens, you will need to have written rules. Involve the children in creating the rules. The more they are involved, the more inclined they are to follow them.

There needs to be some fundamental rules for behavior for younger children. Quiet voices indoors, no running indoors, how to get your attention, when to say "Thank you," and how to share with others are all rules that you can teach your children. Teens need different rules. They need to have rules for when they can use the internet, and how they can use it. They need to be taught how to use privacy controls with social networking sites. There also needs to be rules for cell phone usage. This includes no texting or talking while driving, meal times, and during family meetings.

Sexting occurs when kids send or receive nude photographs of themselves via their cell phones. There needs to be harsh penalties for this within the home. In some states, this is considered a felony crime that can have life long repercussions.

Involvement

Have you ever gone to stay at a friend's home and you weren't allowed to help at all? You watched while your friends did everything! They thought they were doing you a favor by not giving you anything to do, but by the fifth day, you were bored and felt useless. That's what can happen to your children if you don't allow them to be involved.

Children love to do things for themselves. It makes them feel responsible and respected. Every time they try out something new and master it in their own way, they feel better about themselves. A major key to good self-esteem is an "I can do it!" attitude. That is the attitude of a "winner"--someone who can and will surmount all obstacles to achieve success.   That is the attitude that your children need to have.

Find ways for your children to become involved. They enjoy little jobs and bigger ones. Young children love to take out trash, dust, help with dishes, and to help with food preparation. They like to do things for themselves, like dress themselves, feed themselves, and go to the bathroom alone. What a sense of accomplishment they receive as they do these tasks. If your children are not used to doing these things for themselves, and are old enough to do them, you will help them to get an "I can do it!" attitude when you encourage and nourish all steps in this direction. Remember that they have a need for order, so something new in their lives needs to be introduced slowly with lots of nurturing as they master each new skill.

Give younger children choices. It is a self-esteem booster for children to choose from a sampling of books, which one they will hear, or from a sampling of clothes, which clothes to wear, or from a sampling of songs, which song to sing. Don't give them a whole closet from which to choose their clothes. They are not ready for that. They are still children. Prepare them for the day when they will be able to choose their own clothes by giving them choices from a selection.

Give older children and teens responsibilities. Divide up household tasks and involve them in choosing several for them to do. When they are driving, they can help with shopping for groceries. Make sure you set limits on how much they can spend. It's best if they have a shopping list.

Stay in charge. Help them to become independent by allowing them to make choices and decisions. Let them experience the results of their decisions. That is how they will learn to be self-sufficient.

Fun

Children have a need for fun. They need to laugh and play. They can't be serious all the time. They need to be children and act like children. Childhood only comes once. It is a time for fun and games.

What a joy it is to be around children. You have the golden opportunity to play and be like a child yourself. You will still maintain their respect. You will still be in charge. Yet, you too, will can have fun.

There are too many children who are growing up too soon. Look around and you will find children who are doing adults tasks. Here's a story to illustrate this point.

Stacey was 9 years old when her parents started treating her like she was an adult. She was very serious. Her parents talked to her as though she were an adult and involved her in all of their day-to-day decisions. She dressed like an adult by wearing make-up, jewelry, and

23

the clothing of an adult woman. Stacey was very proud to be dressed like an adult and treated like an adult. But when Stacey reached adulthood, she felt that she had missed something very important in her life. She had missed being a child, laughing, playing, and acting silly. Because she missed out on this, she didn't know how to play and have fun. She was known as a "wet blanket" around her friends. Stacey became resentful and had to enter therapy.

Childhood is a short stretch of life that can be a joy. It is a time to learn and grow and stretch one's wings. Children need to be allowed to create, to laugh, to play, and to have fun. A child's laughter is like hearing a brook's wonderful spraying sounds. Encourage your children to let go, to laugh, to play, and to be spontaneous. When children say something funny, laugh with them. When they do something silly, laugh.

In my home when my children were growing up, we started a tradition of playing games at breakfast and lunch. They loved those games. Their friends would come over and watch. As my children grew into adolescence, the games continued, but they were different. The games became ping pong tournaments or watching my children playing in school athletic games like basketball. These family times were fun and filled with laughter.

It will help if you laugh at yourself too, when you say something funny or when you do something funny. You are the role model, the teacher, the guide for your children.
Have fun!

THE NEEDS OF CHILDREN

Here is a quick quiz for you to check to see how much you learned. If there are some areas that are weak for you, re-read that section and take the quiz again when you are through. Mark each statement with a "T" for True or an "F" for False.

_____ **1.** It is fine to tell children they are "bad" when they misbehave.

_____ **2.** Children should be sincerely complimented at least once daily.

_____ **3.** "I believe in you!" is a great true statement to say to a child.

_____ **4.** It's not important to be accepting of a child when the child misbehaves.

_____ **5.** Children need a set routine each day.

_____ **6.** It takes courage and strength to be consistent.

_____ **7.** Children do not need order in their environment.

_____ **8.** Children copy what they hear the adult say more than what the adult does.

_____ **9.** Children need an adult who takes charge and gives them freedom within limits.

_____ **10.** Rules are not good for children.

_____ **11.** There are some areas that children enter because they are "red light areas."

_____ **12.** The best way to teach rules is to tell them to children.

1-F 2-T 3-T 4-F 5-T 6-T 7-F 8-T 9-T 10-F 11-F 12-F

CHAPTER **2**

THE REASONS CHILDREN MISBEHAVE

Children misbehave for a variety of reasons. Often when you find the cause of the misbehavior, it's easier to deal with the behavior. The causes give you vital clues of shifts you can make to prevent misbehavior from happening before it happens. The following is a list of some of the most common reasons that children misbehave.

Boredom

Boredom is the number one cause of misbehavior for children of all ages whether they are young toddlers, preschoolers, or whether they are adolescents. Children need movement, stimulation, and activity. Everyone does. Have you ever gone to hear a speaker and felt bored? You may have had the urge to walk out. You may have had the urge to giggle. You may have started doodling or talking to a friend. You may even have started to fall asleep. It's the same with children. Even more so!

There are some times that you may expect your children to sit still while you are talking. Here are tips for speaking in such a way that your children are never bored. Start with being enthusiastic. Enthusiasm is infectious. If you are excited about what you are telling your children, it will rub off onto them. They will catch your excitement.

Make eye contact. Children mistakenly think that if they don't look at you when you are speaking, they can pretend they did not hear you. That is why it is so important to make eye contact.

One of the things I like to do when I'm speaking to children is to do something unexpected to hold their attention. I will pop on a silly hat, make a silly statement, or just laugh and be silly. Young children love this, but the interesting thing is that so do teens. When I break out in song while speaking to them, they look at me like I'm a bit goofy, but they sure do listen, and sometimes, they break out in song in response to what I said.

Another very important way to hold their attention is to vary your voice tone. Sometimes speak softly, sometimes loudly, sometimes talk quickly, and sometimes slow it down. They typically pay the most attention to a quiet dramatic voice. Children can't listen to you if they don't know what you really want them to do, so it's important to "hook them" when you speak.

Children typically get bored when there is nothing stimulating happening. In today's media generation, it's more important than ever to have stimulating, fun opportunities for children. Have toys around that hold the attention of younger children. I have seen children who are totally reliant on their parents playing with them or holding them. Children need to learn to do things for themselves with age appropriate toys and games. Find toys and games that they can play with independently and get that good, "I can do it" feeling without your help or intervention.

Older children need stimulating activities, too. Teens are often self-absorbed thinking (dreaming) about peers and relationships. They find it boring to sit and talk when it's so much easier via cell phone or internet. Reach the children where they are. Find your own fun ways to using safe media.

Children get bored if something is too easy. They need the challenge of something new and exciting, something that takes some concentration, and something that they can master. If it is too easy, they may get the feeling, "Why bother! Anyone can do that." They also get bored if something is too hard. There's a special frustration of knowing you cannot possibly do something. The attitude then becomes, "Why even try." And when that happens, the children stop trying.

As children get older, boredom can create bigger problems. They may get on the internet and get involved with things that are dangerous. There are many temptations in school and socially. Prepare children ahead by creating open communication so that they feel free to tell you things that are on their minds.

"Keep the doors to communication open."

Trying Out New Behaviors

It's a normal part of development for children to feel bursts of independence and try out new behaviors. They need to be encouraged and allowed to do this as long as it is safe. Sometimes, children are not told that something is wrong to do. They look at adults as models and want to copy everything that they do. Take the example of this young child, Megan, coming into her mom's bathroom and watching her mom put on make-up.

Mom stands in front of the mirror and starts by putting on some foundation, then make-up. She adds some blush. As she puts on each new item of make-up, she smiles more. She likes the way she looks. Megan is standing nearby, unseen, watching. Mom adds eye shadow, eye liner, mascara, and lipstick. She smiles at herself happy with the way she looks. She is ready to go out.

What about Megan? She's been standing there watching her mom in the mirror. Her mom looks happy and pretty. Megan doesn't know that she is not supposed to put on make-up. She only knows that it looks like so much fun.

The next morning when Mom walks into the bathroom, she sees Megan sitting on the bathroom counter in front of the mirror putting on her mommy's make-up.

Was Megan misbehaving? No. She was just trying out a new behavior. This happens often. There are many other examples. Four-year old Ethan tried to shave his legs, Cyndi tried to bake a real cake while her mom was sleeping. Cory saw his dad's cigarettes and lighter on the table, and lit a cigarette and started smoking it. William took a beer out of the fridge and drank it. Children copy what they see and don't think of it as misbehaving. That is why it is so important to be and do everything you want your children to do.

> **Be and do everything you want your children to do. They are watching you and learning.**

Problems in the Home

Often children hold in their feelings and behave inappropriately as a method of releasing their feelings of frustration, hurt, and anger. It's hard to hold in feelings. Here is an example of little Bobby, and the all too frequent occurrence in young children's lives — divorce.

Bobby senses that something is going on at home between his parents. They don't seem happy anymore. They walk around the house looking angry, and they barely speak to each other. When they do speak, they yell. Bobby doesn't know what is going on. He feels the tension in his home and the frustration. He gets scared. He thinks that he has done something wrong. Sometimes, children like Bobby try to hold their parents marriage together. When they fail, they feel like they are failures. When children think that they are bad, they will start to behave that way. Bobby acts all right in his home, but when he gets to school, he acts out.

Parents typically want to shield their children so they don't say anything to them when something serious is happening. This increases the problem. Children are smart. They can sense when something is wrong. It's much better for children if they are told what is going on. They do not need to hear all the details, but they do need to be reassured that they are not to blame. If there is a separation or divorce, parents need to reassure children that they had nothing to do with the marriage terminating.

There are other similar situations that may cause tension in the home. Perhaps one of the parents is ill and needs surgery and wants to protect the child by keeping it a secret. Perhaps, both parents are thinking of a pending move to another city and are not ready to talk about it. Perhaps one of the parents is concerned about losing a job. All of these are stress areas. Children sense the stress and tension, typically act normally within the home, but then act out, releasing their frustration and tension outside the home.

Weather Changes

Anyone who has worked with children for awhile can tell you that children get tense and more easily frustrated before the weather changes. Provide lots of movement opportunities for young children to let out their pent-up energy.

When there is bad weather, and children are stuck indoors for long periods of time, they need lots of outlets. I live in Houston. We have had hurricanes and severe weather in which we had no electricity. Children still need those outlets whether there is electricity or not. They have tons of pent-up energy to release. It's frustrating to have to stay inside all of the time. Be sure and give children lots of other outlets if they have to stay indoors. Have lots of movement games and bring the "outdoors" inside.

Children's Needs Not Being Met

In an earlier chapter, you learned about the importance of meeting the needs of children. These needs must be met in order for children to thrive. When these needs are not met, children may misbehave.

Observe your children. Do they feel loved? Is there structure in their lives? Are adults consistent? Are adults following through with what they say to children? Are there wise adults whom the children respect? Do the children have boundaries? Do they feel involved and important? Are they having fun? These are all needs that must be met in children.

Allergies

There are children who are sensitive to sugars, dyes, food additives, and high carbohydrate foods. These children will act differently and be much calmer if these foods are eliminated from their diets. Observe the children after they eat. Is there a difference in their behavior? If there is, there may be a food sensitivity.

Children can "overdose" on sugar. Children may misbehave after eating ice cream, cake, and cookies. This is one reason that children will misbehave after Halloween or a birthday party. These high sugar foods give the children a lot of energy. When the energy wears off, they become tired and irritable.

There have been documented cases of hyperactive children that were allergic to either foods or air-born substances. When these were eliminated from children's environments, the children became calmer. An allergist can best diagnose if this is the case with one of your children.

Fatigue

Children need their rest. Preschool children function best if they have early bedtimes. Preschool children should get at least 10 hours of sleep each night. That often means going to bed by 8:00 p.m. Elementary school-aged children also need lots of sleep. They require 8-10 hours. Teens need plenty of rest too. Their bodies are shifting and changing, and they will be better able to control their moods if they are not tired.

Children can get used to less sleep, but that is not what they really need. They need lots of sleep. Sleep is like food for children. It nourishes them and helps them to revitalize. Tired children are crabby and much less cooperative.

"Children and adults need plenty of sleep to function best."

Hidden Message to Boys that "It is Okay to be Aggressive"

When a boy misbehaves parents sometimes say, "Isn't that cute? He's all boy." When they say this, they are unintentionally reinforcing his negative behaviors. The best way to prevent this is to make sure that you never give any approval to misbehavior.

Children Who are Bullied

Bullying is becoming more and more of a problem. Children that are victims of bullying may act docile in school, but may come home and act out. Being bullied is similar to being abused. Children that are abused, often have negative self-images. They may become angry children with low self-esteem. Children with poor self-esteem are much more prone to have behavior problems.

Children who are abused may react one of two ways. They may retreat inwardly. These are children who seem to be "loners." These are children with thick walls around them who retreat within those walls. They hold in all that they are feeling. They become depressed and withdrawn. This is a dangerous place for children to be. When the communication stops on the outside, it's time to be very worried about what is happening on the "inside."

> **When the communication stops on the outside, it's time to be very worried about what is happening on the "inside."**

Another way that children who are bullied may react is to become angry. Children may take their anger out on their parents and their siblings. They are feeling helpless and powerless at school, and they let their anger out in areas where they don't feel there is danger. They feel safer at home. If you have a child who is uncharacteristically angry, look for the cause. If the cause is bullying, it is important to take action to protect your child.

Overindulged Children

Parents typically love their children very much and want to give them everything they can. Often these parents want to give their children what they did not have when they were children. Parents generally have less time than in the past. This creates a situation in which parents often feel guilty that they are not spending enough time with their children. As a result, parents try to "make it up" to their children. They do this by providing more and more material items, as well as allowing their children to have many privileges.

Parents may set up unreasonable expectations for themselves. When they can't meet these expectations, they feel guilty and try to make it up to their children. The more they try to make it up to children, the more they give. The more they give, the more the children become demanding. Children begin to feel and act like they are "entitled." They can become "all about me" kids who think that the world revolves around them. They want what they want, when they want it. When this doesn't happen, they become frustrated and angry. They may have tantrums, scream, withhold love, hit, and/or act out, to get what they want. The more their parents give in, the more the children learn that their inappropriate behaviors work. They learn they can get what they want by acting out. It can become a vicious cycle for parents. They set a boundary, and the child does not like it and acts out. The parent sticks to the boundary, and the child's inappropriate behavior escalates. Eventually, the parent becomes worn down, and just gives in. The child has learned, "If I hold out longer than you, I can get whatever I want."

It is important to end this cycle. Children cannot have what they want whenever they want it. It is unrealistic. They will not learn to be respectful and responsible.

Illness

Children who are ill are naturally crankier. Aches, pains, or fever are taxing on the body. Children cannot always verbalize that they are ill. They just know that something feels differently.
Observe children closely. A clue may be a sudden change in behavior. Another clue may be that children hold or touch parts of the body that

aren't normally touched. For example, children with ear infections frequently hold onto their ears.

Children who are ill and hurting may misbehave. What children need is caring and rest until they have recuperated. Most children need reassurance. It's frightening to be ill at any age. Medications that children take because of illness may cause side effects such as hyperactivity or its opposite, lethargy. Be sensitive to the medications that your children are taking.

Normal hormonal changes that occur during adolescence can result in changes in the behaviors of children. Help children understand the changes happening. It is frightening for them when they feel more moody and temperamental.

Negative Behaviors Have Been Reinforced

Children learn to misbehave when their negative behaviors have been reinforced. Reinforcement may be defined as giving attention to a behavior in such a manner that it increases the likelihood of the behavior recurring. For example, when a child hurts another child, if you give a lot of attention to the negative behavior with words and with acting shocked, the child will have the misbehavior reinforced. The likelihood of the child doing the same thing again will be increased.

Here's a story to illustrate this point. I had just finished speaking in a small town and was hungry, so, I stopped in a little roadside restaurant to get a snack on my way home. I was relaxing at a table, when a family walked into the restaurant and sat at the table next to me. It was a mom and dad and their little boy who looked like he was about two-years old. He had nothing on except a diaper, and the diaper looked "fully loaded." His little body looked like he could have used a bath. His hair looked sticky and dirty. His parents were talking to each other, and he sat there, and then started pulling on his dad's shirt saying, "Daddy, Daddy." His dad just ignored him, and the little boy tugged on his dad's shirt even more, saying, "Daddy, Daddy." His dad finally turned toward him very angry and "smacked him." Just before the child started to scream out in pain, he gave a tiny inward smile. He had his negative behaviors reinforced. This little child had learned that attention of any kind was good. He was grateful for his dad's "heavy hand."

Sometimes, a child will say a 4-letter word. When an adult becomes shocked, and the child sees that shock, it can be a reinforcer for the child to do it again to get that same shocked reaction. Therefore, you have to be very cautious with you words and actions when children misbehave. The very behavior that you want to eliminate may actually become reinforced by your reaction.

Media

Children enjoy watching television. Often the programs that they watch display inappropriate behaviors that children will attempt to duplicate. When children watch violence and sexuality, they may attempt to duplicate these. Studies have validated that children who watch violence will frequently act out in a more aggressive manner. Therefore, it is important to monitor the television programs that children watch. It is not only violence and sexuality that can cause misbehavior. Some of the comedies on TV have humor filled with put-downs and sarcasm. Children learn to engage in the same inappropriate behaviors when they watch these programs.

It is not only television that can foster inappropriate behaviors. Video games, computer activities, and music can be contributors. When children play video games in which they "kill" others, they are learning that it is easy to kill someone and not feel badly afterwards.

The use of media is not bad. It's how it is used or abused by children that can create problems.

"The more you connect, the less you correct."

THE REASONS CHILDREN MISBEHAVE

Here is a quick quiz for you to check to see how much you have learned. If there are some areas that are weak for you, re-read that section and take the quiz again when you are through. Mark each statement with a "T" for True or an "F" for False.

_____ **1.** Fatigue is the number one cause of misbehavior.

_____ **2.** It's important to be enthusiastic with children.

_____ **3.** It can be boring to have something too hard.

_____ **4.** You can prevent children from trying out new, inappropriate behaviors if you tell them ahead the areas that are taboo.

_____ **5.** When there is tension in the home, children sense it and may think it is their fault.

_____ **6.** Children may become tense and easily frustrated before the weather changes.

_____ **7.** When children's needs are not met, they may misbehave.

_____ **8.** Some children are sensitive to certain foods, dyes, and food additives.

_____ **9.** Sugar is good for children because it gives them the lift that they need.

_____ **10.** Preschool children need 8 hours of sleep nightly.

_____ **11.** Television does not affect children's behavior.

_____ **12.** The less consistent the adult is, the more the child will act out.

1-F, 2-T, 3-T, 4-T, 5-T, 6-T, 7-T, 8-T, 9-F, 10-F, 11-F, 12-F

Chapter **3**

DEFINING POSITIVE DISCIPLINE

Discipline is very different from punishment, yet often these concepts may be confused. Discipline is used for TEACHING correct behaviors. It is a much more positive approach than punishment. Punishment is concerned with PENALIZING behaviors. Children learn better when they are taught rather than when they are penalized. They learn through being firmly, lovingly, patiently, and calmly taught. The result is that children have a greater knowledge of what is expected, what their limits are, and feel a sense of security because their world is orderly.

A major difference between discipline and punishment is that discipline is concerned with future behaviors. The focus is not on the misbehavior of the present, but of ensuring that children understand that inappropriate behavior cannot occur in the future. That is very different from punishment. Punishment is concerned with behavior that is occurring in the present or in the past, not with the future. It doesn't concern itself with building future positive behaviors. It simply is a statement of "I won't tolerate what you did."

When punishment is used, the adult is typically frustrated and angry. The child senses the frustration and anger and has several choices, fight or flight. Children who go into the flight mode surround themselves with protective walls to protect themselves. They withdraw into this protective walled shell and hear nothing the adult says. Afterwards, adults may think to themselves, "Did my child hear a word I said?" Some children do not go into a flight mode, but instead go into a fight mode. They become angry and belligerent. They may argue more, and the battle may escalate. When punishment is used, children may become resentful. They may vow to themselves to "show" the person who punished them that they can get away with inappropriate behaviors, and the behaviors can occur over and over again. Contrast this to discipline. When positive discipline is used, the adult is calm and firm. Children pay more attention to what they hear when adults are calm.

When the punishment is over, adults sometimes feel guilty and think, "Did I come on too strong?"   They may even go into an atonement mode in which they give in to children for other inappropriate behaviors.

Look at the chart below to see the differences between discipline and punishment clearly defined.

DISCIPLINE

PURPOSE: To teach correct behaviors

FOCUS: Future

ADULTS EMOTION: Patient, calm, firm, loving

CHILD'S FEELING: Security, self-control, wisdom, positive esteem

---

PUNISHMENT

PURPOSE: To penalize for misbehavior

FOCUS: Past or Present

ADULTS EMOTION: Anger, frustration

CHILD'S FEELING: Guilt, anger, fear, insecurity

Chapter **4**

Five Steps Toward Positive Discipline

Step One: *Cool Down*

Never discipline when you are angry. It automatically becomes punishment. You can use any of the positive discipline techniques that you will be learning, but if you are angry, it will still be punishment. The reason it becomes punishment is because the child automatically goes into fight or flight mode. You will be teaching your child fear or anger for incorrect behaviors. This is opposed to teaching your child future correct behaviors.

It is normal to get angry. It would be amazing if you never did get angry. It is how you handle your anger that is important. You need some powerful quick and easy ways to cool down.

Take a mental time-out; a power pause. Take a deep breath. Think about something peaceful. Slowly exhale the anger. Do it again and again. Each time you inhale, inhale peace and calm and strength. Each time you exhale, release the anger and frustration. Do this until you "feel" all of the anger is dissipated. It's great if you can do it in a place where your child can watch you. You will be teaching your child a powerful way to deal with anger. You will be teaching your child that it is okay to be angry, and how to cope effectively with anger.

One of my favorite strategies for cooling down is to go to your "magical place." Try it now. Remember something that is very relaxing for you. It might be a special place. It might be a special time in your life. It might be with someone in your life. Picture that special place. Let yourself remember how good it felt. Take some deep breaths and then come back to this place. That is all it takes—a few seconds of remembering something pleasant in your life to cool down.

Some people like to pause for a second and touch something like a religious object or something special. I know one person who touched her heart as a reminder to just calm down and remember that her children were loved by her regardless of how angry she felt. She said it was an instant calming technique for her.

When you are "cooled down," you are ready for the next step in positive discipline.

Step Two: *Think about an Appropriate Response*

It is always best to act rather than to react. Now, that you are calm, think about the situation that made you angry. Is it something that warrants discipline? Is it something that should be ignored?

Perhaps, you have a child that is used to being penalized, who thinks that he or she is bad. It would be better to ignore as much as possible this child's misbehavior and instead, focus on positive behaviors. It's time for this child to start feeling good. Focusing on the negative will result in more negative behaviors.

> **Whatever you focus your attention on, will expand.**

Perhaps the child was simply trying to get your attention. Children who have their basic emotional needs met are getting attention so, it may be that a basic need is not being met for that child. What need can you meet now? Look at the environment. Is it developmentally appropriate? Does the child have good self-esteem? Does the child have special needs? Does the child have friends?

Think, think, and think some more. Trust your intuition. Look at the family dynamics. Decide which discipline and guidance technique would be most appropriate for this child at this time. The next chapter in this book is packed with strategies for you. Your goal is to eliminate misbehavior and build a positive self-image in that child.

Step Three: *Choose the Right Time and the Right Discipline Strategy*

It is best to use positive discipline and guidance strategies immediately after misbehavior has occurred. However, there are times that this may not be possible. If a child misbehaves and then realizes it and becomes scared, wait until the child is calm. Tell the child that you are waiting in a patient and loving, yet firm manner.

Be careful of the setting for discipline and guidance. Make certain that children do not feel embarrassed. Children are very concerned with what others think. They become embarrassed when disciplined in front of their friends. Remove children from settings in which they may get embarrassed.

Using the Bedroom

If you are in the home, it's best not to use the child's bedroom for discipline. That is a place for peaceful sleep, not a place for learning new behaviors. When children are sent to their rooms, they are inadvertently rewarded for misbehavior. They go to their rooms and get on their cell phones, the internet, watch TV, or if they are younger, play with their toys.

Step Four: *Believe in Yourself*

Children are smart. They can sense if you are hesitant and uncertain when you speak to them. If you don't believe in your own ability, they won't believe in it either. It's that simple. If you are with children, and have an "I don't think I can handle this attitude," they will sense it, and you will not be able to do it. It's important that children have someone they respect, someone who makes wise decisions. They need you to believe in yourself.

If you believe in yourself, you will automatically appear more confident and assertive. Children can sense in your voice tone and in your posture whether or not you feel strong in what you say. They sense whether or not you believe in yourself and whether you believe that you can succeed. If they feel your confidence, then they will listen to you.

It takes a change in attitude. Your attitude has to be, "I can handle any situation. I can do it." This book will give you great strategies, and those strategies will help your confidence. However, it will still be up to you to believe in yourself. That is the key to having children believe in you. That is the key to respect. Think of people you respect. They most probably are confident. They believe in themselves. They are happy and fulfilled people. They know "they can do it," and therefore they DO IT. Now is the time to turn your attitude around. You can do it.

Step Five: *Believe in the Child*

Children need to have someone who believes in them. They need to have someone who accepts them and sees beyond inappropriate behaviors. They need someone who sees their positive characteristics, too. If you see the positive traits in children, they will begin to see them.

Children are much more than their inappropriate behaviors. Each child has a unique and special personality. The child's personality can get stifled and colored by the expectations and beliefs of others. Sometimes, children hurt inside. The hurt may be covered up with misbehavior or through retreating inside a shell that is like a coat of armor.

Children need to be nurtured. They need to have someone to believe in them. The more you believe in the inherent goodness of children, the more they will start to see it within themselves. You will see a change in their behavior that will amaze you.

This may take a shift of attitude within you. It may mean nurturing and believing in a child whom you have not believed in before. It's easy to believe in children that do everything right. It's not as easy to believe in children who can't seem to do anything right. These are often children in whose lives you can make a huge difference.

Jess was like this. He lived with his grandparents and his mom. His dad left when he was young. He had no privacy at home. Both of his grandparents drank too much every night. When they drank, they often started yelling at him and his mom. Financially, his mom needed to live with them, so she was afraid to move out. She was so tired at the end of each day that all she wanted to do was go to the room she shared with Jess and watch television. She didn't stand up for Jess. Jess started to act out in school. He made more and more inappropriate choices and was constantly sent to the office. One day, his counselor met with his mom. They had a long talk and his mom told the counselor what was happening at home. The counselor explained how Jess needed someone to believe in him, and the yelling at home was wearing him down. His mom decided to make some changes. She moved out of her parents' home into a tiny apartment with Jess. Every night they spent time together talking about their days, and they became really close. There was an immediate improvement in Jess' behavior. He had his mom now, someone to believe in him.

Children are more sensitive than they may appear. They need to be nurtured. They need to be believed in. The more you believe in the inherent goodness of children, the more "good" they will be. You will see a change in their behavior that will amaze you.

> **Whatever you focus your attention on, will expand and grow.**
>
> **Focus on the good in children, and it will expand and grow.**

Billy was a child who always got mediocre grades. Everyone thought that he was a mediocre student. His family and his teachers all thought this was true. Even Billy thought so. Finally, when Billy was in high school he had a teacher who said to him, "You can do better." No one had ever said those words to him before. Now he had someone who believed in him, someone who believed that he could and would do better. He did! He started getting all "A's" and "B's." Today, he is a successful international financial consultant. This is because of the power of someone who believed in him, one teacher who changed his whole life.

Mary was emotionally and physically abused at home. She acted out at school and in public. Mary screamed out for attention, because she didn't feel loved. Her Aunt Jessica moved nearby. Aunt Jessica believed in Mary. She believed that Mary could do and achieve anything. Aunt Jessica saw through Mary's inappropriate behaviors to the little hurting girl who simply needed love and someone to believe in her. Mary completely changed. She started taking pride in herself. She started walking with confidence and talking with enthusiasm. Mary went to college and became a social worker helped other people. This was all because of one person who believed in her.

Here's a touching story about the difference an early childhood teacher made in a child's life. It illustrates so vividly the power of believing in a child.

Four year-old Jonathon had huge eyes, curly hair, and seemed to never smile. He lived with his grandma, who was very old and not very healthy. Jonathon's mommy had died when he was two years old. No one knew who his daddy was. Jonathon came into child care every morning wearing the same outfit almost every day—a faded but clean t-shirt, a pair of dark green pants, old worn tennis shoes, usually mismatched socks, and a sad look.

It would have been easy to feel sorry for Jonathon because of his circumstances, but Jonathon also walked in the door every morning ready for a fight. He walked up to the children, and if someone was sitting near a toy he wanted, he just shoved the child out of the seat. The kids were all scared of Jonathon, his temper, and his tantrums.

His teacher, Miss Betty didn't really like him at first. He was just one of the difficult kids in her class. She wanted all of her kids to be easy to work with, but, she knew she had to do something different with Jonathon. She had to get through to him. He was at an age where if he kept this up, he could get worse and worse as he got older. She didn't want to "write him off." She started watching him to see what held his attention. She looked for his likes (which were very few) and she looked for his dislikes. She found that he had more dislikes than anything else. She was having a really tough time not disliking him, but, she kept at it. That's what she was there for—to make a difference and Miss Betty was one determined woman.

One day, Miss Betty came into school in a really great mood, humming the song, "Side by Side." She noticed little Jonathon looking up at her with those big brown eyes. She started singing it a little louder. *"We ain't got a barrel of money; maybe we're ragged and funny, but we'll travel along, singing a song, side by side."*

Jonathon edged up to her, and for the first time, she saw a little smile on his face. He took hold of her hand which was a first, and started singing with her, *"We ain't got a barrel of money; maybe we're ragged and funny, but we'll travel along, singing a song, side by side."* Miss Betty was so amazed that she sang it over and over again. His smile grew and grew. From that moment on, Jonathon and Miss Betty became close buddies. Jonathon remained at her side. She didn't ask him any questions, just enjoyed his wonderful behavior. One day, about a month later, Jonathon and Miss Betty were sitting together out on the playground during recess, and little Jonathon got really serious. He looked up at her with those huge sad eyes and said, "My mommy used to sing that song to me. We used to sing it together every night before I went to sleep. Miss Betty, I have something really important I want to ask you." Miss Betty said, "Sure Jonathon. You can ask me your question." Jonathon said, "Miss Betty, Can I call you mommy sometimes?"

Miss Betty nearly started to cry. She said "Yes, Jonathon, you sure can. I am not your real mommy, but I will be honored to have you call me "mommy.""

The years passed and little Jonathon grew. As he went on to elementary school, middle school, and high school. He always stayed in touch with Miss Betty. When he got a driver's license, he would drive over to the child care center, and they would have lunch together. Miss Betty was very proud of him. He graduated from high school and was voted "most likely to succeed." Miss Betty sat in the front row watching him receive his diploma. When he went away to college, he wrote to her keeping her updated about all of his activities and classes. When he came back to town, he always stopped in at the child care to see her. Miss Betty never did marry. She stayed in child care, loving her work.

Jonathon graduated from college and graduate school and got a great job in another state. He always stayed in touch. One day, Jonathon received a phone call from the owner of the child care center. She said that Miss Betty was very ill with leukemia and was in the hospital. She told him that she thought he would want to know. Jonathon thanked her and got on a "red eye" flight that evening, flying all night just so he could see Miss Betty the next day.

He arrived early the next morning and went straight to the hospital. He asked where her room was and was directed to Room 324. He looked inside the room, and saw a tiny sleeping figure on the bed surrounded by tubes and medical paraphernalia. It was Miss Betty. She was so frail, and he could see that she was very ill. He walked up to her bed, and she opened her eyes and saw him. She smiled the biggest smile. He bent down to gingerly hug her. They hugged and held each other. He said, "Hi Mommy." She was so happy to hear him once again call her that. She looked up at him, and weakly said, "Can we sing it one more time?" He knew immediately what she was talking about. They held hands, and he sang to her,

"Oh we don't have a barrel of money; maybe we're ragged and funny, but we'll travel along, sharing a song, side by side."

Just like Miss Betty made a difference in Jonathon's life by believing in him, that's what you need to do, too. Never, ever give up. Always believe in them, and you will make a huge difference, traveling alongside children, creating your own songs as you touch their hearts and change their lives.

SUMMING IT UP

Following these five steps toward positive discipline will completely change the way that you and children relate. These are the foundation for not only effective discipline, but for more effective living. You will teach children how to deal with anger when you "cool down." You will also teach them to trust their own intuition as you trust your intuition. They will trust you more because you are careful to choose the right setting and the right time for discipline. Your belief in yourself will provide them with a strong sense of security as well as give them respect for you. Most importantly, your belief in your children will give them what they need most to function in the world. You will remind them of the goodness that they each can be. In turn, you will benefit also! You will become strengthened each time you use these five steps. You will believe more and more in yourself, your abilities, your own strength, and your own goodness.

WHAT IS DISCIPLINE AND FIVE STEPS TOWARD POSITIVE DISCIPLINE

Here is another quick quiz for you. If there are some areas that are weak for you, reread that section and take the quiz again. When you have 100%, you will know you have really "got it!" Then, you will really be able to use it with your children. Mark each statement with a "T" for True or an "F" for False.

_____ **1.** Discipline focuses on the misbehavior of the past.

_____ **2.** The adult's emotion during discipline is anger and frustration.

_____ **3.** The child feels secure and learns self-control and understanding when discipline is administered.

_____ **4.** It's okay to feel angry when you discipline your child.

_____ **5.** "Cool Down" is Step One toward positive discipline.

_____ **6.** Sometimes, if a child is frightened after misbehaving, it is better to wait to use positive discipline.

_____ **7.** Whatever you put your attention on, will decrease.

_____ **8.** Embarrassment is an effective discipline tool and should be used as frequently as possible.

_____ **9.** Your attitude has to be, "I can handle any situation!"

_____ **10.** If you believe in yourself, you will be confident.

_____ **11.** It's better to spend your time believing in the child who rarely misbehaves, who does everything right!

_____ **12.** Children need to have someone in their lives who accepts them and who sees beyond any behaviors to their essential goodness.

1-F, 2-F, 3-T, 4-F, 5-T, 6-T, 7-F, 8-F, 9-T, 10-T, 11-F, 12-T

Chapter **5**

101 Solutions for Discipline Dilemmas

"Do something, and when you have done something, if it works, do it some more, and if it doesn't work, do something else."

--Franklin Delano Roosevelt

This is a quote by Franklin Delano Roosevelt from the 1932 Baltimore Address. This quote is as relevant today for discipline and guidance of children as it was in his day with the subject matter he was talking about. There are no magical discipline strategies that can be used over and over again that always work. What works one time with a child, may not work again. What works for one child, may not work for another child. What works for one parent or teacher, may not work for another parent or teacher. What works for one situation, may not work for another situation. That is why it is important to have a variety of discipline techniques to handle all situations.

This section is designed to give you many effective strategies to help you with children. The more often you read them, the more familiar you will become with them, and the easier it will be for you to find the perfect discipline and guidance strategy when you need it.

> **"What works for one child, may not work for another child. What works for one parent or teacher, may not work for another parent or teacher. What works for one situation, may not work for another situation. You need many strategies."**

Positive Discipline and Guidance Strategies for All Situations

1. Establish Eye Contact

If you shout across the room at a child, you are teaching YELLING through role modeling. When the child is misbehaving in another room or in another part of the same room, walk over to the child. Get down on the child's level and look right at the child. Quietly and firmly tell the child *not what is being done wrong*, but what it is that you want. Look into the child's eyes and make sure the child is looking at you. Children often don't want to make eye contact because then they think they can pretend that they did not hear you. If a child looks away when you are looking at the child, say very quietly and firmly, "I know that you can hear what I am saying." Look directly at the child even when the child doesn't look at you.

2. The Serious Look

When a child is misbehaving, stop what you are doing, and give that child a very serious look. Your look needs to convey to the child the message, "You may not do that now." It should be firm enough so that the child will immediately stop the behavior.

When I am doing workshops, I have the participants pause and take turns practicing the serious look. It does take practice. Once you have it mastered, children will immediately stop what they are doing when they see the look on your face.

3. Redirect the Child

Many times, children who are mischievous simply need to be redirected toward another activity. This is the positive approach. It will help you avoid words like "No," and "Don't." A child who hears "no," and "don't," over and over again will start to say those words. Here is an example of redirecting children.

The Situation	The Redirection
Little Cathy is getting ready to touch the wall plug.	Cathy's mom says, "Cathy, I need you to come here. I have something that's fun for you to do."
Michael is being argumentative about an issue at school. His mom is cooking dinner and wants him to become calm.	Michael's mom says, "Michael, I need some help for a few minutes with this pot. It's too heavy for me to lift."

There are similar situations that happen in school with teachers. Miss Thomison has a preschool child named Daniel in her classroom who is mischievous. Daniel moves near two children playing with a toy. Miss Thomison knows from past experience that he will probably try to take the toy from the two children.

The Situation	The Redirection
Daniel is getting ready to take toys away from other children.	His teacher says, "Daniel, let's play together with these new blocks."

Miss Albertson teaches secondary school. Kaley is one of her students who has problems sitting still. Kaley is getting ready to go sharpen her pencil (which is very noisy) for the third time.

The Situation	The Redirection
Kaley is getting ready to get up for the third time to sharpen her pencil which is a distraction for the class.	Her teacher says, "Kaley, I need you to do an errand for me."

In each case, the behaviors have been redirected, and negative statements that would have lowered the self-esteem of children have been avoided. This is a simple way to divert children from misbehavior. Give children something more fun and more stimulating. You will stop the misbehavior in its tracks.

There may be times when children are trying to tell you something with misbehavior. For example, young Thomas may be spending too much time in the bathroom. He loves to play with water, and he uses every opportunity that he gets to splash around with water. Distract Thomas by getting out a basin of water and a few spoons and scoops. Thomas can play outside in a designated area with the water. The activity does not have to be related to the misbehavior. It can be something completely different. The important thing is that it is stimulating and fun for children so that they want to do it.

4. Laughter

Sometimes, the behaviors of children are genuinely funny. Think about it. It's amazing what their minds can conjure up. Some situations with children are as hilarious as any comedy television program. Have fun. Enjoy yourself. If children are not deliberately trying to get in trouble, just join in, laugh, and have fun.

When you do laugh, make sure it's not sarcastic. It's important that children do not interpret your laughter as making fun to them. Instead children see that you are simply enjoying the uniqueness of the situation.

5. Consequences

A consequence is a direct result of misbehavior. For consequences to be effective, it is best for them to be related to the act. For example, if a child frequently spills their beverage at meal time, the logical consequence is for the child to clean it up. It may take the child longer than it would take you to clean it. It may not be as clean as it would be if you did it. However, the child will have learned to take responsibility for the behavior.

It's important to be patient when using this technique. Children work at a slower pace, so it will take longer for them than it would for you to clean up any messes. Gently, encourage children along the way, especially if it is a long and difficult situation to fix.

I had a student in my school who decided to be mischievous. One day, he went into my office while I was in another room. He took a tiny bottle of white-out and started "painting" my room. He "painted" the desk, the door, a tiny table in the room that held a coffee pot. He even painted the coffee pot. I never realized that there was so much fluid in that little tiny bottle!

When I walked in the room, he had the open bottle of white-out in his hand. He took one look at my face, and he started yelling, "I didn't do it. I didn't do it."

To say I was upset is to put it mildly. I had just finished decorating that new office. I knew I couldn't talk to him right then. I had to cool down. I did some of the cooling down strategies that you learned in an earlier chapter, and then I could talk. I told him that I would wait for him to calm down, and then we would speak. He was pretty hysterical saying all kinds of things and waving his arms around. He knew he had been caught in the act.

When he finally did calm down, we talked, and I told him he would need to clean up the white-out. He came in early for several weeks to clean it all up. We got to form a really close relationship in the process.

The goal of a consequence is not to punish, but to teach children to be responsible for their actions. Be cautious of the way you speak to children so your voice is caring, yet firm so that children know that you will follow through.

6. Overlooking Negative Behaviors and Complimenting Positive Behaviors

This is the easiest technique of all, but it can be the most difficult to do. The reason for this is that it calls for INACTION when there is inappropriate behavior. This is a strategy used when children misbehave because they have learned it is one sure way of getting attention. This is a negative form of behavior that children have learned. They become accustomed to engaging in negative behaviors and then getting reinforcement (attention) for it.

This is particularly true of children who think they are "bad." These children are used to engaging in negative behaviors and constantly getting reinforced with attention for the inappropriate behaviors. You can end the cycle by ignoring these behaviors, whenever possible. When you pay attention to the negative behaviors, you are inadvertently reinforcing the beliefs of children that they are bad. You are reinforcing their faults rather than their strengths.

> # Whatever you focus your attention on, will increase.

Find the positive strengths in children. Sincerely compliment these strengths. This will help children realize that they have strengths. Slowly, but surely, it will increase their self-esteem.

This does not mean that you should ignore all misbehavior especially if a situation is dangerous. This is an effective strategy for reversing a pattern. Some misbehavior needs other strategies. That is why this book is filled with strategies. Use your judgment as to when it will work best.

Here is an example of a situation in which this would be effective. Young Patrick won't eat what his mom has cooked for him. This is a chronic problem. His mom struggles to come up with foods that Patrick will eat. Patrick is even bribed with special desserts if he will eat. The negative behavior of Patrick not eating is being reinforced with lots of attention. Therefore, the negative behavior increases daily.

Here's what will work. DO NOT give Patrick dessert or any other snacks if he does not eat his food. Do involve him ahead of

time, by giving him choices. "Would you like to eat _____ or
_____?" In that way Patrick is empowered by having
participated in the decision-making process. Be sure to compliment
Patrick when he eats what he has chosen.

Tattling

Tattling is a very real problem. Children tattle on other siblings,
tattle on friends, and tattle on adults. Generally, when a child tattles,
the adult steps in and solves the child's problems. This provides a
temporary solution until the child tattles again.

A tattle is defined as occurring when a child tells someone in
authority what someone else did. A tattle is not to be confused with
reporting. There is a major difference between these two concepts.
They each have very different goals. The goal of reporting is to get
help. That help can be for the child who has a problem or for
someone else. The goal of tattling is to get someone in trouble.
Children need to be taught these differences.

The following tools are effective when the child is using tattling in
order to get another child in trouble. They are not to be used when
the child really does need help. That is the reason why it is very
important to teach children the difference between tattling and
reporting. Once you have looked at the reasons the child is tattling
and conclude, there really is no reason, the following techniques can
be used. Some of the first techniques are ways for you to determine if
there may be a reason.

7. Sounds Like

This is a really great response to children, especially if you are
not sure it the child is going to tell you a tattle or report a situation that
needs help. Listen to the child, and if it is a tattle, use this response.
Use the words "Sounds like….," followed by the feeling that you are
hearing from the child. For example, if the child is upset, say, "Sounds
like that made you upset." If the child is angry, say, "Sounds like that
made you angry."

This is a great way of acknowledging the child's feelings about
the tattle without getting involved in resolving the issue for the child.
Typically, the child will walk away happy to have been heard. If the
child still wants to get the other child in trouble, respond with a
question. "What do you think you ought to do now?" This puts the
onus back on the child to resolve the problem.

8. Tell the President

Have a photo on the wall of the current President or a former President. The child tells the President the tattle.

Lincoln

9. Tattle Ear

Have a photo of an ear on the wall. The child tells the ear the tattle.

10. Tattle Time

Have a special time each day for tattling. If a child has a tattle earlier, the child waits until tattle time to tell it.

11. Tattle Sandwich

This is a really neat strategy. The child first must tell you something nice about the other child, then the tattle, and then end with something nice. The tattle is "sandwiched" between the compliments. This teaches the child that it is important to look for good things in others, too.

12. Tattle Box

The child writes or draws the tattle and puts it into the tattle box. At a special time each day, all the tattles are taken out of the box.

13. Tattle Stop Sign

Hold up a stop sign when the child begins to tattle. Ask the child if the tattle is a report or a tattle. Put the Stop Sign down if it is something to help the child or to help another person, the child can tell the tattle. If it is not, have the child use one of the other techniques like the tattle ear.

14. Chronic Tattler In Charge

If a child tattles all the time, the child may not really realize how it sounds. Put the child in charge of hearing all tattles. The child will get so tired of hearing tattles, that the child will stop telling them. This is especially effective in the classroom.

15. Tattle Form

This is a technique for older children who can write. Have a form that the tattler needs to complete. It takes a lot of time to do this and eliminates a lot of tattles before they happen.

Tattle Form

Tattler's Name_____

Tattlee's Name_____

Date_____

Time_____

Tattle_____

_____

Result of Tattle_____

_____

A Better Way to Handle the Situation would be:_____

_____

Signature of Tattler_____

Signature of Tattlee_____

It's important to remember not to reward tattling by getting involved or by punishing the other child. If you jump into the fray on the tattler's side, there will be more tattles. You will be reinforcing the tattling behavior, and the tattler will have achieved the desired effect. You also may be unfairly punishing the other child. The biggest effect is that you will be teaching the tattler that tattling is an effective way to get someone else in trouble.

Power Struggles

Power struggles can be draining. They become a battle that no one wins. Experts give credence to what many parents and teachers instinctively know -- that many children have in-born traits, such as being exceptionally strong-willed. As these children grow older, so too do the power struggles.

It's also important to note here that there are times that power struggles are more developmentally appropriate, and that is with two groups of children, toddlers and teens. Each group is hard-wired to test the waters of independence. They are on a teeter totter one moment saying and acting, "I want it my way," and the next moment, wanting to be held and comforted like a small baby. Understanding those factors is key to knowing what solution is likely to work in any given situation.

For instance, a parent or teacher can back away from a request to have a child participate in an activity if the child is balking and the adult feels like this is a battle best left alone. But the adult doesn't always have that option. There's no wiggle room when it comes to situations regarding health and safety, such as when a child doesn't want to abide by rules that can impact the child's safety.

16. Don't Argue

Instead of trying to gain the upper hand with a strong-willed child, get calm. It's important not to see the child as an all-powerful little person who is out to make you miserable. Instead, it is important at all times to realize that this is still a child—a child who is forming patterns that will last a lifetime. The child needs your guidance to manage his or her behavior.

Keep in mind that you are the adult. You are the one in charge. When you become engaged in a "battle," there is always a winner and a loser. It becomes like a war with two countries battling against each other, wanting to win at any cost. The costs can become quite expensive for the countries in terms of human lives. The costs, also, become very expensive in terms of human lives when there is a power struggle. While it is important for you to take charge, it is imperative that at no time, the child loses self-esteem in the process.

> **DO NOT:**
> - Argue
> - Raise your voice
> - Use sarcasm

17. Use Power Talk Techniques

Be brief when speaking to the child. Less is truly more. The more you say, the more danger there is of the child and you getting into an argument. There is also an increased danger of the child simply tuning you out.

Be firm. Have your voice convey that you mean what you are saying. Have your entire body language show that you are expecting the child to comply. This may take practice. You may want to practice in front of a mirror. You can also record yourself. Listen to yourself on the audio or video tape. As you listen, think to yourself, "Would I listen if someone spoke like that to me?" "Was I firm, yet did I convey that I cared?" Those are important concepts you want to ensure that the children sense as you speak.

Be clear in what you say. Use simple age-appropriate words that the child understands. Sometimes, you may think the child understands, but the child heard what you were asking in a totally different way. For example, you might tell a child to put the cell phone away. The child puts the cell phone on the table. In the child's mind, that is putting the cell phone away. Instead, clearly say, "I need you to turn the cell phone off and put it in your room." When you clearly describe what you want done, there is a better chance that the child will comply.

Go to the child when you speak. It's important to not shout across the room. If you are speaking to a younger child, squat down to the child's level to tell the child what it is you want.

Use pauses as you speak for emphasis. For example, say, "Jordan, (pause), I need (pause) you to put that book (pause) on the shelf."

Use a low deep voice and have your voice get deeper and lower with each word you say. The lower your voice, the more the child will listen.

Say the words, "I need" rather than "I want" or "You should" or "We need to." The words, "I need," are a much more powerful way of speaking to the child.

18. Co-Create Rules

Enlist children's help in creating their own rules. Interrupting a strong-willed child who is busy with something, by saying, "It's time to clean up," in an authoritative voice, is almost certain to create a power struggle. But if the children have all helped create rules that include a chart that designates children do particular chores each day at a certain time of day, you can refer to the chart when it's time to clean up. Then the chart, not you, becomes the one in charge, and power struggles can be deflected.

Sit down with children and come up with rules together. The more they are involved in creating the rules, the better the chance they will participate in following them.

19. Provide Two Positive Choices

This is a very important strategy for handling strong-willed children. They like to feel that they are important and that their decisions matter. Frequently, because of temperament, their whole world revolves around themselves and getting what they want when they want it. It is generally not effective to say to a strong-willed child, "You do this or else!" They balk! It is also ineffective to offer a positive choice or a negative consequence. For example, it's best to avoid statements like, "Pick up the books, or you will have to clean up the whole area." Instead, it is better to offer two positive choices. "Parker, I need you to pick up the books or to straighten up the kitchen. Which do you prefer?" Once the child tells you, be sure and say, "Thank you."

Here are a few more examples of two positive choices. "Patricia, would you like to sit down in that chair or this one?" "Colin, would you like the green beans or the corn?" As you read this, think of situations in which you have gotten into power struggles and think of what you could have said instead.

20. Read Body Language and Redirect before the Struggle

Learn the telltale signs of a power struggle about to take place. Then try to head things off by distracting and redirecting children For example, Stevie folds his arms across his chest and shakes his head no when he's about to say no to something. Seeing this happen, the adult distracts him with a book. "Stevie, I found that book you have wanted to read. Would you like to look at it now or do you want to look at it after lunch?"

21. Calm Down

The importance of becoming calm prior to discipline has already been discussed. However, it's important to remember that in order to handle power struggles and strong-willed children, you must be calm. When you lose it, the children lose it, too. Actually, when you lose your "cool," the child has just won the power struggle. The child has won because, regardless if the child gets what he or she wanted, the child DID get to see you lose it! That reinforces a game that children often will continue playing called, "Get the adult!"

22. Laugh Together to Stop Power Struggles

Sometimes being silly is just the trick for breaking through a power struggle in the making. It definitely gets the attention of children when you are joyful. If you have an older child or teen who is getting argumentative, you can simply laugh, and playfully say, "Again." If a young child's face has become tense and serious, one fun game is to play "Find the Smile." Have the child look around the room to find smiles. The child looks in shoes, out the window, magazines, under a table, and in a mirror until the child and you are smiling and laughing.

23. Use Novelty

Children love novelty. Do something unexpected to change the entire mood of the room before any power struggles develop. Stand up and sing or dance. The more fun you are having, the less power struggles you will have.

24. Have a "Wise Choice" Chair

This is a voluntary place that both you and the children go when you are feeling you need to make a wise choice about something to prevent a problem. It is a nice comfy chair. It might even be a rocking chair. It could also be a couple of cozy pillows on the floor.

Sometimes, there is just so much going on in life that it can get difficult to think straight. When the child goes to the "Wise Choice" chair, the child thinks about all of the options available and then strives to choose the wisest one. This is a great strategy because you are teaching the child to pause and reflect before they engage in behavior.

25. The Paper Bag Trick

When there is a power struggle, instead of arguing with the child, ask the child to tell you all the things that he or she can do that are appropriate. You and/or the child, write each choice down on a piece of paper. Put them all into a bag. The child lifts one out of the bag and that is the child's choice for that situation.

26. Whisper into the Child's Ear

When a child is really upset and argumentative, calmly whisper into the child's ear. First, it is distracting to the child that is on a tirade to have you whisper. Secondly, the quieter your own voice, the quieter the child becomes. Thirdly, it is very calming for the child when you are calm and whispering. The child gets quieter and quieter as the child listens intently to what you are saying.

27. Re-Channel Their Strengths

Children who are strong-willed generally have great leadership abilities. They know how to persevere. This is shown when they hold out to get their way.

They know how to "read" people. They intuitively seem to sense where people are more sensitive and vulnerable. They often choose just the right time and place to make their arguments—these are times where the adult will not be as strong.

They know how to manage others. Because they are so strong, others generally heed them. Take advantage of this and harness the leadership ability that strong-willed children have. Redirect them to doing projects that help others. Involve them in creating ideas. You are actually training them to use the gifts they have in a much more appropriate way.

28. Get Creative

Take a totally unexpected approach to shake things up. For the young child who repeatedly refuses to come to the lunch table, enlist the child's help in following a line of imaginary caterpillars to the table. If the child is older, it becomes a little more challenging. Yet, you still can get creative. Talk "teen talk." Put yourself into the older child's shoes and think about what works. If you want the teen to help with a chore, have the child listen to his or her favorite music at the same time. Make it more fun to do the things that need to be done.

29. Make Fewer Requests

It has been found that children may be on the receiving end of up to 40 requests from adults in an hour. This is an overwhelming amount for anyone. After awhile, children tune adults out. Reduce the amount of requests to the really important ones.

30. Use Gestures and Props to Show What You Want

Some children are visual or tactile learners. They really don't understand what you mean when you give auditory instructions. Use visual cues to help children understand what you want. You can gently place a hand on a child's back to help guide the child somewhere.

31. Repeat

When you run up against resistance from a child—especially a young child, mirror what the child says, by repeating it back. When Samantha says "No, no, no," repeat her words back to her and add, "No, no, no! You don't want to go inside!" Pause for emphasis, because you've got her attention now. Repeat, "No, no, no," and add, "You don't want to go inside. I understand. It really was fun. It is time to go inside now for lunch."

For older children who say, "No way!" to a request. Say, "No way….you don't want to do that. I understand. Okay, you can do it now or wait 3 minutes. Which do you prefer?"

32. Use "Regardless" and "Nevertheless"

When a child starts to battle with you, simply listen to what the child says. Then calmly and firmly say, "Sounds like you want to…, nevertheless, I need you to …." Here's an example. Jamil is pushing and pushing to stay outside when it's time to come in. Very calmly say, "Sounds like you are upset. Nevertheless, I need you to come inside now." You can substitute the word "regardless" for the word "nevertheless."

33. Teach Children to Say "Okey dokey"

Play a fun game. Make a request and children respond, "Okey dokey." Here's an example. "It's time to clean up and get ready for lunch." Young children respond, "Okey dokey!" They love it. It feels more like a game than an order.

34. Be Understanding, but Persistent

The child who resists you by telling you that he or she wants to stay outside for five more minutes or draw one more picture needs you to be understanding, but persistent. "Emily, I know that you want to stay outside. You will get to go outside later. I need you to go inside now." To the older child, "Toby, I know you want to stay up later and stay on your computer, but I need you to turn the computer off and turn the lights out now."

Children Not Following Directions

Children of all ages often want to do what they want to do, when they want to do it. They need to learn that life does not work that way. In life, there are times that they get to do what they want to do, and there are other times that someone else is in charge, and they have to follow directions. If they get on an airplane, and they decide they are not ready to have the pilot take off, the pilot will still take off. Here are some tips to get children to listen better and follow directions.

35. Use Anticipatory Cues

Some children have a difficult time with transitions. When this happens, they can tend to be disrespectful by not following directions. Provide special cues so that children know what comes next. A bell is a good way of doing this. Ring a little bell ahead of time so that children know a transition is coming up. For example, ring the little bell, and then say, "Soon, it will be time for lunch." This strategy not only works with younger children, but it works with adults. I have attended meetings for adults, and the leader rang a little bell to get the attention of a diverse group. It worked. Everyone stopped talking, and the meeting began.

36. Give Warning

It helps when you tell children ahead of time that an event will take place. "In 10 minutes, it will be time to put away the computer and video games and come eat dinner."

37. Use Proximity Control

Always stand near the child when you ask for something. Never shout across the room. Your presence, your close proximity, is a gentle reminder to follow directions and also to engage in more appropriate behavior.

38. Use Checklists

Some children are very visual. Give them a checklist of items to do. Make sure that it is not overwhelming by being too tough or too much. Children do the items on the checklist, check them off, and then at the end of the day, they return them to you. The checklist is effective with older children and teens. It will work with younger children in a modified version. Rather than having a checklist of written items, have a task card with pictures of items for the child to do.

39. MBWA

The letters, "MBWA," stand for "managing by walking around." This is an effective technique for business managers. It also is effective for parents and teachers. It does not mean sticking your nose into everything children do. It does mean being involved, and walking around. In your home, you may find that your child is watching something on TV that is inappropriate. In your classroom, it shows children that you are on top of things.

40. Give Clear Directions

Here are some directions for you. *Take your left hand and make a circle with it. Now put your thumb in the center of the circle.* Those are very unclear directions. It is not clear whether or not you are to draw a circle with your left hand using a pen or pencil, or whether you are to just form a circle using the fingers of your left hand. It is not clear whether or not you are to use your right or left thumb in the center of the circle. It is easy to give unclear directions to children, too. Be very careful when giving directions.

41. Avoid the word, "Don't"

Here are directions for you again. "Don't picture a pink elephant." My guess is that you probably pictured a pink elephant. Children pay more attention to the rest of the sentence, then to the word, "don't." Here are some examples: "Don't yell." "Don't run."

Children hear the verb, the action word, and do what you tell them not to do. Instead of using the word don't, use the "power talk" strategy that you learned earlier. "Catherine, I need you to…." That will work much better.

42. Change Your Voice

Have you ever gone to hear a speaker, and the person spoke using the same voice tone the entire time? After awhile, you probably tuned the speaker out. Children will tune you out, too. Vary your voice, sometimes speaking faster and sometimes slower.

43. Lower Your Voice

When you want children to listen to you, you may speak in a loud voice. Children tune out yelling and shrill voices. They pay better attention to a lower more dramatic voice.

44. Use a Prop to Get Children to Listen

It's fun to use props to get children to listen. They will often listen better to a puppet telling them what to do then to a person even though the person is making the puppet move. Find your own age-appropriate prop for children.

45. Use Music to Get Attention

Children respond to music. Have special music you play when you want children to stop what they are doing and listen to you. One mom asked her teenaged daughter, who never listened, what song she could play that would get her to listen. Her daughter told her one of her favorite songs, and it worked. This works for all ages and for both parents and teachers.

"Never give up."

Complaining

There are some children who complain all the time. They say, "I can't" and actually stop trying to do things. They complain when you ask them to do chores or complain about family outings. They whine and complain. Here are some strategies for you to use.

46. Change "I Can't to I Can"

Sometimes children complain about doing things because they are afraid they won't do well. Tell children stories of people who refused to believe they could not! Tell them about Beethoven who was deaf but composed beautiful music.

47. Have an "I Can't" Box

Have children make a list of all the things they cannot do. They drop it in the box. Take the box, and toss it. Tell them it's like throwing their "I can't's" out the window. They are starting fresh.

48. Erase the Word, "Impossible"

Get a dictionary and look up the word impossible. Cross it out and tell children that from now on, you want them to think about all the positive things they can achieve instead of focusing on what they can't achieve.

49. Have a "Complaint Box"

Children drop their complaints into the box. Read them at a designated time each week. If they are valid, follow through on making a change.

50. Stand Firm

Sometimes children whine and complain as a strategy to get what they want. Little Julie whined and whined when she didn't get what she wanted. I was her teacher. One day I asked her while she was in the midst of whining, "Julie, does that work for you?" She answered, "It works every time with my daddy."

Anger and Tantrums

How Tantrums Start

Tantrums generally occur when children want something and they do not get it. It can be a progression from pouting to whining and/or crying to tantrums. Children may pout when disappointed. If the pouting doesn't work, they may progress to whining. If they get what they want, they learn that this works. When this stops working, they have tantrums. It can be said that tantrums are often a way that children shout out what they want. It is reinforced when they actually do get what they want.

Here's an example. Damon wanted a cookie. He asked his mom for a cookie. She told him "no." She said it would ruin his dinner if he ate a cookie right before dinner. Damon was really unhappy about this. He pouted. He still didn't get what he wanted. He started whining. He said, "You don't love me. I'm starving." His mom still said "no." He whined more, getting progressively louder. His mom finally couldn't stand all the noise. She thought to herself, "This isn't worth it. Just this one time, I will give him a cookie." She gave him the cookie. Damon ate the cookie telling his mom she was a good mom and he loved her so much. When he was finished, he said, "That was so good mommy. I'm still starving though. Can I have another one?" Damon had learned that he could change his mom's "no" to a "yes."

He was a young child. Older children and teens do the same thing. They usually whine with arguments like, "All my friends can do it." "You just don't understand." They whine and argue. They pout and stop talking or they pitch a tantrum, saying things designed to provoke guilt in parents and teachers.

Some children may have tantrums because they see the role models in their lives coping with demands by whining, screaming, and/or raging when they want something. These children learn to do the same thing, to have a temper tantrum to get what they want.

Stress can cause children to act in ways they would normally not act. There are many sources of stress in children. Significant others in their lives may have too high expectations. The children feel they cannot live up to them so they react by acting out with tantrums. Still another source of stress can be fear. Children may be scared of new situations, and/or new people. They react by having a tantrum.

Displaced anger is another reason children have tantrums. They may be angry at others. Carrie was being bullied at school and through social media. She said nothing to her teachers or to her parents, but she started acting differently. She was quick to get angry. She let out all the angry feelings at those with whom she felt safe, her family, and teachers.

Young children may become angry and frustrated. They have less verbal skills to ask for what they really want, so they use a tantrum to tell the adults in their lives what it is they want.

> ***There is usually a reason for everything.***
> ***Discover the reason***
> ***and you are half-way home to the solution.***

Strategies for Tantrums

Children are each different. What works for one child may not work for the next child. Not only are children different, but, so too, are the adults in their lives. It is very important for you to be comfortable with the technique you use with children. Therefore, you will learn a variety of techniques to handle tantrums. Take time to think about the individual child, the reason for the tantrum, and you will find the strategy that works best. Remember, if at first you do not succeed, do try and try again. You hold the keys to helping the child learn more appropriate behaviors.

51. Answer Calls for Help

If you suspect that the child is crying out for comfort and love, give this to the child. This does not mean to give in and reverse a decision you have made for the child. That would be inconsistency. It simply means showing the child that you care. Instead of becoming impatient, listen to the child.

52. Acknowledge the Child's Feelings

Sometimes, a child just needs to hear that you understand what the child is feeling. Acknowledge the child's feelings. Say words like, "I can see you are angry."

53. Teach the Child to Use Words

Teach children to talk about what is bothering them rather than acting on it. Help children realize they will not get into trouble for being angry at someone or something. Instead the child can say, "I'm really angry," or "I'm really sad." The more the child can express verbally, the better the child can feel. This does not mean that the child will automatically get what he/she wants, but that the child has a right to have feelings and to express them. This is a healthy tool you can teach children that will last them their whole lives.

54. Change the Mood

Start singing a song. Talk about something exciting that is going to be happening. Play a fun game. Instead of paying attention to the tantrum, simply do something different.

55. Have a Tantrum Mat

This is a strategy for younger children. Sometimes the best way for the child to feel better is simply to have the tantrum. The child needs a safe place to do this so that the child won't get hurt or hurt anyone else. Show the child a special mat that is kept in a very special place. Explain that if the child needs to have a tantrum, to go get the mat, put it in a special place, and have the tantrum. When finished, the mat is returned to its special place.

56. Teach Deep Breathing

Breathing deeply is calming. When children are upset, they breathe shallowly. The more shallowly one breathes, the more anxious the child becomes. Teach children to breathe deeply, inhaling into their abdomens, holding their breath for a few seconds, and then exhaling slowly out through their mouths.

57. Use the Paradoxical Intervention

This is a great strategy because it empowers the child. Have the child choose ahead what will work if the child is upset. For example, the child may choose a special place in the room like a rocking chair and the child may also choose to have a comfort object while sitting in the chair. When the child starts to get upset, the child goes to the special place to calm down before there is a tantrum.

58. Have a Relaxation Station

Set up a comfy place that is calming. Have some comfort objects depending on the age of the child. Have a rocking chair and even headphones to block out noise and distractions. The goal is to have the child go to the Relaxation Station to calm down instead of having a tantrum.

59. Use a Pocket Comfort Item

Holding a special object can be comforting. A little photo of a loved one or even a superhero can be comforting and prevent tantrums before they ever occur. The child gets out the comfort object and looks at it until calm. In place of a photo, it can be a religious token or something else that is calming for the particular child.

60. Use Distraction and Redirection

There are times when you can predict that a temper tantrum is brewing. When you see this happening, you can often nip it simply by distracting the child with something else to do. Here's an example: "Oh my gosh, did you see that!!!! Wow! Let's head over there and see it closer up." At the same time as you are redirecting to something else more appropriate for the child at that moment, you are also distracting the child from being upset.

61. Do Exercise

Physical activity releases tension. Younger children can do "laps" within the home. Create a circle on the floor that is marked with colored tape so it is clearly visible. The child walks around the circle for laps until calm. Older children can go jogging, play basketball, or other exercise.

62. Teach the "Turtle Technique"

Talk to children about turtles. When turtles get upset, they withdraw within their shells until they are calm. They don't yell or scream or have a tantrum. When they are calm, they start moving again. Children can do the same thing. When they are upset, they do not act out. Instead, they retreat for a little bit until they are calm again.

63. Push the Pause Button

Have a special television remote control that is not hooked up. Show children the remote. Teach them that when they are upset and think they may need to have a tantrum, to calm themselves by getting the remote and pushing the pause button until they feel better. They can also deep breathe at the same time. Children find it comforting to have a tangible way to stop tantrums.

64. Lower Your Voice More and More

When you are talking to the child, lower your voice more and more and more. The lower you get, the more the child is surprised by the difference in your voice tone. This is an effective form of distracting the child from having the tantrum.

65. Use Books

Books are a vehicle for becoming calm. They are mood changers. When children are upset, they can read one of their favorite books until they feel better.

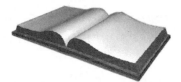

66. The Magical Rocking Chair

There is something magical about sitting in a rocking chair and rocking. It is relaxing. Have a comfy rocking chair for children to sit in and rock back and forth until they feel calm.

67. Draw Anger Away

Drawing is a wonderful way to express feelings for children of all ages. They draw or paint their feelings, and it provides a safe release.

68. The Joy of Journaling

Journaling your feelings is a wonderful way to release anger. When children write about the situation, they see it more objectively, and start to feel better. Older children need to be able to do their journaling privately.

69. Use Calming Words

You play a big role in calming children. Your attitude and your words are a calming influence. Your mood is contagious. The calmer you remain, the calmer children can become more quickly. Here are some calming statements for you to use:
"I see that you are upset. It's okay to be angry."
"What is something you can do to feel better?"

70. Mirror, Mirror on the Wall

Sometimes children do not realize how they are feeling until they see their own faces. Invite children to look in a mirror to see visually how they feel. Tell them to try and think of something that makes them smile.

71. Music Relaxation Pillow

Have a special pillow that is soft and comfy. When children are upset, they can hug the pillow and listen to calming music at the same time.

72. Squeeze and Relax

Teach children to scrunch up their hands tightly for a few seconds, and then release and relax. They do this several times until they feel better.

73. Positive Self-Talk

Teach children to say positive words to themselves when feeling upset. "*I can do it. I am okay. I can handle this. I don't have to get angry.*" When children feel themselves becoming angry, they use "Self-Talk" until they feel calm.

74. Have a Bug Box

Have an empty box labeled, "I am bugged." When children are angry, they write down the things that are "bugging them" and put them in the bug box. The adults can do this, also.

Younger children do a variation of this. Have a box filled with cute little pictures of bugs. When the child is angry, the child expresses the anger by going to the Bug Box, pulling out a Bug, and handing it to whoever is "bugging" him. The child says, "I am feeling bugged." It's a simple way to have children express their feelings.

75. Feather Duster

Have a feather duster in a special reserved area of the room. When children are upset, they get the feather duster and dust themselves off until they feel better. They dust off the negative mood. Younger children love this. It is even effective for adults.

76. Stressbusting Stress Ball

Have a stress ball. Children squeeze the stressbusting ball until they feel better. If you don't have a stress ball, they can squeeze a sheet of scrunched up paper.

77. Role Model Self-Control

Children copy what they see. Be careful how you handle your own anger. The more they see you model self-control, the more contagious that will be for them.

78. Anger Log

This is a form that children complete after they have become calm. It is a way for them to learn to handle their behavior better. They write down what happened, and they rank the intensity of their anger. They write about how others saw their anger, a more appropriate way they could have handled the anger, what they can do now to make it better and what they can do in the future when they get angry.

79. Anger Rules

Teach children anger rules. Here are good rules.

It's okay to be angry, *but*
- Do not hurt someone
- Do not hurt yourself
- Do not hurt property
- Do talk about it.

80. Compromise is Good

Compromising is an important skill for children to learn. It can go far to prevent defiant angry behavior. Teach children that each person has their own version of a conflict, and to come up with a middle ground whenever possible.

Bullying and Cyberbullying

Bullying is becoming a bigger and bigger issue. It is a recurring issue that negatively affects many children. It is a serious problem that can leave long-lasting scars that affect children years later. It affects not only the victims, but also the lives of the children who have seen it, as well as the children who bully. It is important to stop bullying.

Bullying is defined as <u>repeatedly</u> harming others who have difficulty defending themselves. The key word here is "repeatedly." This is not just a once or twice occurrence. It is something that happens over and over again. Cyberbullying is using the internet or cell phone to send hostile messages to someone or about someone. It can become vicious. It typically occurs with teens, but it can start even younger.

There are some important strategies to help children.

81. Teach Children to "Tell"

First and foremost, teach children to "tell." Children typically do not tell their parents or their teachers. They don't tell for several reasons. They feel embarrassed, and think they can try and handle it themselves. Bullying typically escalates. It is not something for them to handle alone. They need help.

Another reason they don't tell adults, is they are afraid that adults will make the situation worse. It is important to make it safe for children to tell about bullying. They need to know that the adults in their lives can be trusted to help them, and the situation will get better, not worse.

82. Do Not Minimize the Bullying

There are incidents in which parents and school officials knew about bullying, but did absolutely nothing. Bullying is serious. It can lead victims to carry out dangerous acts of retribution to others. It can lead to depression and even suicide. Take bullying reports seriously and do something. Doing nothing is doing something, the wrong thing.

83. Be Persistent Helping Victims

If you hear about bullying, do not simply tell someone and pass the buck. Don't stop helping victims until the bullying is actually stopped. Go higher and higher to get help even if it means reporting bullying to local authorities.

84. Teach Bystanders to Take Action

Bystanders witness the bullying. They may even take part in it out of fear that they, too, may be bullied. That escalates the problem. Teach children that if they are bystanders, they need to report the bullying.

85. Keep Confidentiality

The greatest fear of victims is escalation of the bullying. It is vital that even though you take action, you keep as confidential as possible to protect the victim.

86. Teach Children Privacy Settings

Older children enjoy using social media. Teach them how to have privacy settings to help prevent cyberbullying. If there is cyberbullying, report it to the designers of social medial, such as Facebook. They can take steps to stop it. Make sure that children save all bullying messages.

87. Cell Phones

If children receive cyberbullying messages, make sure that they save them. Parent and guardians need to report the problems to their individual telephone companies. Block any numbers that are problems. Change the child's phone number if needed.

88. Teach Empathy through Questions

Empathy is the opposite of bullying. It is the ability to identify with and understand how another person feels. It is the ability to put yourself into someone else's place. It is important to have empathy in order to build positive relationships. The more children can identify with the way others are feeling, the less likely it is that they will bully.

Children need to be taught to empathize not only for those people whom they know in their families, but also for others. Ask questions such as: "Is it okay to hurt an animal? Is it okay to hurt people? Is it okay that people hurt other people on television?"

Help children who bully others to focus on the victim's feelings. This helps them to learn to think about others before they impulsively act. Some other good questions are:

"How would you feel if you were new in school?"
"How would you feel if you wore thick glasses?"
"How would you feel if someone said bad things about you?"
"How would you feel if you could not speak English well?"

89. Teach the Child How to Be a Positive Leader

Children who bully others frequently have other children copy them. They are leaders to these children, and the children do what they tell them to do. Sometimes, it is because of fear, and sometimes, it is because they are admired. Using this technique, you acknowledge the child's leadership abilities and give the child opportunities to be a positive leader. You and the child jointly work out a plan to develop these leadership abilities. Have times and situations in which the child is in charge. Oversee the child to help the child develop into a positive leader. Have fun together. This is a great technique. You will both be empowered and get closer through its use.

90. Teach the "Golden Rule"

Talk about the saying, "Do unto others as you would have them do unto you." Ask children to tell you what they think it means. Explain that it means that you treat others the same way that you want to be treated. Everyone likes kindness and caring.

91. Inappropriate Language – 4 Letter Words

Young children don't know that there is anything wrong with saying "four letter words" when they say them. It is the reaction of adults that reinforces the behavior. When adults are shocked and appalled to hear these words, they generally respond with something like, "We don't ever say those words." The adult is calling attention to negative behavior. The more negative attention to the behavior, the more the behavior reoccurs. Instead it is better to ignore the word the first time. It may just be something the child heard, and the child has no idea that it is inappropriate. If it happens again, the adult can respond: "I prefer for you to use another word when you are upset. Choose one now to use." The adult is clearly setting a boundary while at the same time empowering the child.

Older children sometimes think it is cool to use inappropriate language. Their peers may be using the same words. It is also important to not be shocked and reactive with older children. Instead, set a boundary stating that inappropriate words cannot be used in your presence. You can also state that you prefer the older child does not ever use those words.

It is very important that you are careful in the words you use. You are a role model, and they are watching and listening.

Biting

Biting typically occurs in children who are under three years old. It is important to immediately disinfect the wound and give attention and nurturing to the victim. Typically, biting begins with a child accidentally biting another child, and the reaction of the adult may be intense--"HOW COULD YOU DO THAT?!!!!" The accidental behavior may become reinforced with negative attention. The more frustrated you will become, the more the child may bite. Therefore, it is important to stay calm when the child bites.

92. Say "Stop"

Firmly say, "stop," and put all of your attention on the victim.

93. Use a Substitute Object

If the child repeatedly bites other children, give the "biter" a substitute object to bite instead of biting another child. It may be a teething type of toy. Have it be an object that the child can carry and use instead of biting. If the child forgets to use it, and bites another child, say, "Stop," firmly and gently. Tell the child to bite the object instead of another child. I like to call the object, a "bitmajig." Children like this name.

94. Have "Yes" and "No" Books

A strategy that is extremely effective is to have two books: A "Yes Book," and a "No Book." The "Yes Book" has magazine pictures of things the child can chew and eat like hot dogs, cookies, and bread. The "No Book" has photos of people and furniture. Show the books to children so they know which objects they can chew and eat, and which ones they cannot.

Whining

Younger children whine, and older children complain. Complaining was previously discussed. Young children may have aches and pains and whine because they don't have the language skills to express themselves. Children may whine because they are genuinely sad. These children need to receive loving care. There are also some children who whine to get what they want. They have learned that if they whine long enough, adults in their lives feel sad or guilty, and will give them what they want. The strategies you will be learning now are for the latter children.

95. The Tear Jar

An excellent technique for children three years old and under, is to have a special jar that is called the "tear jar." Use a small baby food jar or a "shot glass," and put a "Smiley Face" sticker on the bottom. Have the whining child hold the Tear Jar up to his eyes to catch the tears as they fall. The child will probably be startled, yet intrigued. Children like the idea of catching their tears. They like it so much that they generally become distracted from thinking about something they wanted, and stop crying.

96. The Cuddle Bear

When children whine, give them a snuggly stuffed bear to hold. It feels good to hold the bear, and children generally get distracted from whining.

97. 4-H Rug

The 4-H rug is a special rug on which individual children sit or stand when they are whiny, and want extra attention. The 4-H's are: hug, handshake, high-five, and hum. Some children enjoy the physical contact of a hug. Other children prefer less physical contact and want something simple when standing on the rug like a handshake or high-five. Still other children don't want any physical contact, but may want someone to come to them and hum them a song.

"Your own attitude is more contagious than a cold."

Children Who Do Not Follow Through with Tasks

There are some children who have the best intentions, but they get easily distracted or forgetful. There are other children who are simply defiant about following through. There are still other children who do not follow through because they genuinely don't know how to do the task. They may be too embarrassed to ask for help.

98. Contracts

A contract is a great strategy to help children follow through if they are distracted or forgetful. It is also effective with children who are defiant. It gives you a tangible way to ensure tasks are completed. These can be simple chores around the home or homework. In school, this strategy is also very effective for teachers. I used it when I was teaching, and it helped children stay on task.

Explain to children that contracts are used when adults buy a home, car, or other purchases. The purpose of a signed contract is that it is a commitment to complete something. In the case of a purchase, it is a commitment to make payments.

Explain that a contract is a reminder of the commitment. Tell the child that you will have a contract to help the child remember to follow through on tasks, commitments.

Here are 2 contracts, one for the younger child, and another sample contract for an older child.

Sample A: Contract for Younger Child

MY CONTRACT

Child's Name_____

Date_____

I will:

☐ Brush my teeth after I eat

☐ Help prepare snacks

☐ Say "please"

Adult's Signature_____

Child's Signature_____

Sample B: Contract for Older Child

MY CONTRACT

Child's Name_____

Date_____

I will:

☐ Do all my homework starting at 6 pm each night.

☐ Load the dishwasher after dinner

☐ Spend 15 minutes daily talking to my parents with the cell phone and TV and other media turned off.

Adult's Signature_____

Child's Signature_____

99. Give Explicit Instructions

There are children who do not follow through because they do not understand what they need to do. This is a strategy that helps children do the task. There are four steps involved. The first step is to get children enthusiastic about what they will be doing. Talk about it in a positive upbeat way. Secondly, demonstrate by doing the task in front of children. Do it slowly explaining what you are doing as you do it in a sequential manner. Thirdly, have the children do the task with you watching to help them if needed. The last step is to be their cheer leader when they have mastered what they are to do on their own.

100. Involving the Child

The more children are involved in solutions, the more they will want to follow through. Involve children in coming up with completion times of tasks, and the methods they will use to complete the tasks.

101. Regularly Scheduled Meetings

Children need face-to-face meetings with the important adults in their lives. These are one-to-one times. It needs to be at the same time each day. The purpose is bonding and conversation. There are times that children become defiant and don't follow through on tasks because they feel unconnected with the adults in their lives. This can happen with younger children, and it will definitely happen with older children. Teens are busy with their cell phones and internet and their social lives. Have a designated cell and media free time to sit and talk. The conversation will foster bonding. The result is that there is an increased mutual understanding. Children are more likely to follow through on tasks when they feel connected to those who are assigning those tasks.

101 Solutions for Discipline Dilemmas

Here is quiz to check to see how much you have learned. Mark each question with a "T" for "True" or an "F" for "False." If there are some areas in which you are weak, re-read that section, and take the quiz again.

_____ **1.**   Use the same discipline solution for each behavior.

_____ **2.**   "The look" needs to be mean and angry.

_____ **3.**   The contract is used for tattling.

_____ **4.**   Children may whine as a way to get what they want.

_____ **5.**   The 4-H Rug is used for tantrums.

_____ **6.**   The "turtle solution" is for whining.

_____ **7.**   The "yes" and "no" books are used for biting.

_____ **8.**   Avoid the word, "don't."

_____ **9.**   The louder your voice, the more children will listen.

_____ **10.**   The logical consequence of spilling juice is to clean it up.

_____ **11.**   When you pay attention to negative behaviors, you increase the likelihood of them reoccurring.

_____ **12.**   It is okay to redirect a misbehaving child.

1-F 2-F 3-F 4-T 5-F 6-F 7-T 8-T 9-F 10-T 11-T 12-T

Chapter 6

HOW TO PREVENT DISCIPLINE PROBLEMS

Prevention is as important as discipline techniques. If you use the following methods, you can help prevent problems before they ever happen.

Provide a Developmentally Appropriate Environment

Provide for the children's individual needs. The environment needs to be geared toward children, not toward adults. It needs to meet the needs of children so that no child feels frustrated and/or inept. It makes a statement without words. The statement is "You're important. This is your special place."

Be a Positive Role Model

You are one of the most important people in your children's lives. You are a role model, a "teacher," an example for them at all times. You are that role model simply because they are in your presence.

It's imperative that you, "clean up your own act!" If you want peaceful, loving, and joyful children, then you need to be that way. It's a sacred responsibility being in charge of children. It is not something that can be taken for granted. Children can learn behaviors that you dislike within yourself, simply from watching you in action.

They are extremely intuitive. They can sense if something is going on in your life to make you unhappy. They may not know what the unhappiness is about, but they can "intuitively sense" your feelings. They know if you are calm. What is it that you really want to teach your children? Do you want them to learn to be calm and happy? Then, you have to start now to be that way.

Spend time with yourself. Learn to love yourself more and more. The more that you respect yourself, the more your children will respect you. The more they respect you, the more they will want those same qualities that you are modeling for them. You are always a role model. If you are a generous and giving person, they will copy that. If you can receive love easily from others, they will copy that. Therefore, it's important to "be" what you want most for your children. You start it. It all begins with you.

Explain all Situations Ahead of Time

Children have the need to know in advance what is going to happen just as you do. The Table of Contents for this book shows you what will be covered. It's better than having to dig through the book to find what it will cover. There are no surprises. It's the same with children. They too, need to know what to expect.

Prepare children as much as possible for what is going to be happening in their lives. If there is going to be a major change, tell them. They don't have to know all of the details, but they need to know what is happening. They intuitively sense any potential changes anyhow. Tell them about minor changes, too. Are you going to be redecorating a room? That may seem minor to you. To a child who needs structure, that is a major change.

Provide Choices

Children have the need to be independent, yet they really want your approval rather than disapproval. When you provide children with choices, they feel independent, and still are choosing behaviors that meet your approval.

Here's an example. Offer a child a choice of doing several kinds of chores. You are in charge. You are naming the kinds of chores that the child can have. The child is in charge of deciding which he or she wants. You are both empowered. Do the same for clothes, food, books, and movies.

Use a Soft Voice

A soft voice is a powerful technique for preventing problems from happening, or escalating once they have begun. Generally, adults use a loud voice, especially when they become upset. The louder the adult's voice is, the louder the child's voice becomes. Soon, it turns into a shouting match. Use a soft voice with children. Your voice can still be firm while soft. A soft voice is more of an attention grabber if it is firm and dynamic, than a loud voice.

Have a Variety of Rainy Day Activities Available

There are times that the weather is in the process of changing or has just changed. Children have a tendency to misbehave during this time. Be ready for those special days, those days when children need more movement activities. Be on the lookout for new ideas and fun activities for children. Have books that are fun and interesting. Save some activities for those days when children are "antsy." Have some games, crafts, songs, and exercise planned for these days. The more physical movement there is, the better it is for children.

Compliment a Day

Sincerely compliment children for something each day. Make sure that they hear the good things about themselves. It doesn't have to be complex or long. It can be something as simple as saying, "It feels so good to spend time with you." "You are special to me." "I'm glad you're here." That is music to a child's ears.

Tell Children "Thank you" for Appropriate Behaviors

Never let a day go by without thanking children for something they said or did that is appropriate. What a difference that will make in all of your lives. Say thank you to children when they remember to do something that you have asked. Don't always attach the thank-you or praise to a behavior. Sometimes, attach it to the fact that the child is in your life. Each child is so special. Each child brings so much to the world.

Watch the Children's Diets

Diet can influence behavior. Avoid foods that have excessive amounts of sugar, carbohydrates, artificial food colorings, and/or flavorings. They can contribute to behavior problems.

Halloween can be a very difficult time because children eat so much "junk food." Be prepared. Set rules as to what children eat, and when the food will be eaten. Take charge. Do the same for all holidays and special events.

Check labels on the foods you serve. Be careful that children don't see you eat foods that you won't let them eat. Remember, you are a role model.

Have a Positive Attitude

Think positively. If you become negative and think of yourself as weak or unable to handle a situation, that is exactly what will happen. If you firmly and joyfully believe in yourself and your abilities, you will do a better job with children.

Each child is a new challenge. Look at each child as a seed that can bloom into a fragrant flower. Don't look at the flaws of the seed. Think positively about how the seed will look when it is in full bloom, and look for ways for you to ensure that will happen.

Follow Through

When you say something, it is important to follow through. This will help your children to always know what is going to happen. It is confusing for children to hear one thing, and then have it "change" later. They never know what to expect. It's important for children to feel secure. They need to be able to believe in you and your word. Then they will be able to respect you more.

Foster Self-Esteem

Self-esteem is essential. Positive discipline and guidance fosters self-esteem in children. Negative words can deplete self-esteem and confidence. Here is a list of ways to foster self-esteem.
- Help children to be problem solvers.
- Help each child feel important, loved, and wanted.
- Allow children to do appropriate tasks independently.
- Respect each child's feelings.
- Give honest, sincere appreciation for all jobs well-done.
- Make sure that each child feels that he or she has accomplished something successfully each day.
- Sincerely praise improvement.
- Provide encouragement. "You can do it."
- Be truthful and sincere.
- Be tactful.
- Be a good listener.
- Enjoy children. They will sense it and thrive in your care.

CONCLUSION

This book gives you the skills you need for positive discipline and guidance. It is up to you to implement them. Be patient with yourself. This may be something brand new that you are doing. Some techniques and concepts may come easily, and others may take a little longer. Have fun and enjoy yourself every step of the way. That is what is important. Being with children is an art and a skill. It will take as much practice as it would take to learn any new art or skill. You can't learn to play a piano overnight. Neither can you learn to discipline positively overnight. There are keys that you have to learn. There is a melody that needs to be perfectly played. Practice is the answer. Practice, and practice some more, until the music that you play is beautiful. Practice until the relationship you have with children is in perfect tune and harmony. You are a difference maker.